GRAND BANK
SOLDIER

*To Nita,
from Helen
with Love.*

GRAND BANK SOLDIER

*The War Letters of
Lance Corporal Curtis Forsey*

EDITED BY BERT RIGGS

Flanker Press
St. John's, NL
2007

Library and Archives Canada Cataloguing in Publication

Forsey, Curtis, 1895-1993
    Grand Bank soldier : the war letters of Lance Corporal Curtis Forsey / Bert Riggs, editor.

ISBN 978-1-897317-15-0

    1. Forsey, Curtis, 1895-1993--Correspondence. 2. Great Britain. Army. Royal Newfoundland Regiment--Biography. 3. Soldiers--Newfoundland and Labrador--Correspondence. 4. World War, 1914-1918--Personal narratives, Canadian. I. Riggs, Bert, 1954- II. Title.

D640.F659 2007   940.4'81718   C2007-903535-3

© 2007 by Bert Riggs

ALL RIGHTS RESERVED. No part of the work covered by the copyright hereon maybe reproduced or used in any form or by any means—graphic, electronic or mechanical—without the written permission of the publisher. Any request for photocopying, recording, taping or information storage and retrieval systems of any part of this book shall be directed to Access Copyright, The Canadian Copyright Licensing Agency, One Yonge Street, Suite 800, Toronto, ON M5E 1E5. This applies to classroom use as well.

PRINTED IN CANADA

FLANKER PRESS
P.O. BOX 2522, STATION C
ST. JOHN'S, NL, CANADA A1C 6K1
TOLL FREE: 1-866-739-4420
WWW.FLANKERPRESS.COM

Cover Design: Adam Freake

12 11 10 09 08 07   1 2 3 4 5 6 7 8 9

Canada   Canada Council Conseil des Arts
        for the Arts   du Canada

We acknowledge the financial support of: the Government of Canada through the Book Publishing Industry Development Program (BPIDP); the Canada Council for the Arts which last year invested $20.1 million in writing and publishing throughout Canada; the Government of Newfoundland and Labrador, Department of Tourism, Culture and Recreation.

DEDICATION

This book is dedicated to my paternal grandfather, Bert Riggs (1891–1948), a contemporary and friend of Curt Forsey, who died several years before I was born but about whom I have never heard or read any thing that does not indicate that he was a wonderful man.

Taken in Halifax in 1917.

FOREWORD

by Honourable T. Alex Hickman, O.C., Q.C., LL.B., LL.D.

If the English language did not contain the all-embracing word "gentleman," such a word would have to be created in order to properly describe the late Curtis Forsey of Grand Bank. He was a proud Grand Banker, a merchant of princely qualities who never regarded himself as a merchant prince. Curtis Forsey was one of Grand Bank's leading citizens who readily involved himself in the affairs of his hometown and who often cooled a heated discussion into laughter and mirth by his penetrating wit.

The retail store of William Forsey Limited, of which Curtis Forsey was the managing director, was located on Water Street, Grand Bank, next door to Billy Matthews's barber shop. It was in that famous gathering place that fish merchants, banking skippers and foreign-going masters gathered daily for a shave at the tender hands of Mr. Matthews. As a teenager waiting for a haircut I listened with fascination as sea-going skippers told of their experiences on the Grand Banks and foreign-going masters described their visits to foreign ports. The merchants in attendance would knowledgeably discuss world economic conditions and the vagaries of the fish market; the advice of Curtis Forsey and his very profound remarks were given careful attention by those patrons of the barber shop. "Uncle Curt," as he was fondly known in later years, never hesitated to speak to teenagers like myself and, with his devastating wit and his well-deserved reputation as one of Grand Bank's outstanding raconteurs, he would tell me stories of his youth and of the proud history of his hometown.

The letters written home from the trenches of the Western Front during World War I by Curtis Forsey not only show the character of this brave man but are written in such a way as to assuage the concerns and fears of his parents anxiously awaiting his safe return home. One gets the clear impression from reading these letters that whilst facing the withering gunfire of the enemy Curtis Forsey's thoughts were still back home in Grand Bank.

Again, during World War II Curtis Forsey willingly gave his energy and talents on behalf of the war effort. As a member of the Great War Veterans Association he worked tirelessly to raise funds and provide comforts to Newfoundlanders serving in the Armed Forces. His two banking schooners, *Helen Forsey* and *Christie & Eleanor*, were engaged in transporting goods between Newfoundland and foreign ports, often in submarine-infested waters. The *Helen Forsey*, the pride of the Forsey fleet, was sunk by enemy action in 1942 with the loss of two of her gallant crew.

I commend this publication as a salute to a courageous Grand Banker and loyal Newfoundlander who never forgave Canadian Prime Minister MacKenzie King and British Prime Minister Clement Atlee for destroying Newfoundland's independence and creating Canada's tenth province.

St. John's, NL
March 30, 2007

PREFACE

by Bert Riggs

Anatole Broyard (1920–1990), literary critic and book reviewer for the *New York Times* from 1971 to 1989, once wrote *"In an age like ours, which is not given to letter-writing, we forget what an important part it used to play in people's lives."* How true that statement is in an age of cellphones, e-mail, instant messaging and chat lines.

Letter-writing was a lifeline, a source of information and relief, and sometimes of great sadness, for those at home eager for news of their sons, husbands, relatives and friends on the front lines in Europe during the 1914–1918 war. It certainly was for Sarah and William Forsey, who cherished the letters they received from their son Curtis between the time of his enlistment in the Newfoundland Regiment on May 31, 1917, until his safe return to Grand Bank in early February 1919.

Through his letters they learned of his experiences as a soldier in training in Scotland and England, his introduction to the harsh realities of trench warfare, the death of some of his friends, young men from Grand Bank whom they would have known, his joys and his disappointments, his concern for those still at home and for those with him on the front lines. Then came that fateful letter informing them of his injury. It was not life-threatening but it was certainly a cause for concern. He knew what their reaction to the news would be: therefore it is no surprise that his longest and most detailed letter 'takes them through' the events leading up to his getting hit in the ankle and thigh by enemy fire and his subsequent evacuation to hospitals in England.

Forsey's letters contain the thoughts and feelings, some mundane, some poignant, of a young soldier who has volunteered to serve his country in battle. They are first-hand reminders from someone who was actually there, who saw and heard and experienced the tragedy that was World War I. He meant them as private communications for his parents. In one letter he writes to his father *"I'm going to ask a favour of you now. I'm sure you won't though. Don't do as some people do—publish letters they get from their sons. I wouldn't have a letter of mine published for anything and don't tell everybody around town, especially Mrs. Patten or any of those people as they might get excited about it."*

His parents respected his wishes, but they also kept his letters. They were passed down through the family and treated as precious heirlooms of an important event in the life of a son, father and grandfather that must be preserved and remembered. That these letters are now being published may seem to some as breaking faith with Forsey's wishes. To them, I can only say that doing so is in no way a sign of disrespect but a tangible means of honouring him and his fellow soldiers and of making his story available to a much wider audience: to people who want to know and who must not be allowed to forget the sacrifices that so many young Newfoundlanders made on the battlefields of Europe during that war.

This volume includes 51 letters that Curtis Forsey wrote to either his mother or his father during the 19 months that he was on active duty with the Newfoundland Regiment. There are indications in some of the letters that others he had written to them were not received or may have been lost. That is unfortunate but those that have survived do tell an interesting tale.

The transcriptions of the letters have retained Forsey's spelling and grammar; *sic* has been used to identify original misspellings; some abbreviations have been expanded with the missing letters enclosed inside square brackets. Punctuation, mainly periods and commas, have been introduced to provide clarity as these appear to have been less important to him in the cramped conditions under which many of these letters were written. He seldom used question marks and that quirk has been retained. As far as possible the people, places, buildings, events and other references in the letters have been identified, although a few remain elusive or are speculative on my part. Readers are invited to contribute new or additional information or offer corrections for my mistakes.

St. John's, NL
April 26, 2007

INTRODUCTION

CURTIS FORSEY AND THE FORSEYS OF GRAND BANK

The First Forseys

From the mid-1600s, perhaps earlier, the French, who fished along the south coast of Newfoundland, carried out a seasonal fishery from a place they called Grand Banc. They went so far as to establish a small, year-round community, one which lasted until the French were compelled to leave that coast by the Treaty of Utrecht in 1713. This transfer of territory included the island of St. Pierre, to the English St. Peter's, which quickly became their main base of operations along the coast.

Fifty years later, in 1763, the Treaty of Paris, which brought an end to another of the French-English wars of that century, returned ownership of St. Peter's to France, forcing the several hundred English residents living there to find new homes. Many of them made the short trip across the bay to Grand Bank, boosting its small English population and enriching its potential to become one of the leading fishing communities along that coast.

In the 40 years between 1763 and 1803, the increase in the population of Grand Bank was almost fourfold, rising from 53 to 198. A number of individuals and families decided to settle there during that period, each making a unique contribution to the development of the community. Two of these new settlers had a great deal in common: each was from the English county of Dorset, each was named George Forsey, each was married to a woman named Esther. The union of their families would result in a composite family of Forseys, one that was destined to play a leadership role in the political, economic, religious and social life of the town down to the present day.

The first of these George Forseys was from the Parish of Netherbury in Dorset, where he was baptized on April 17, 1848. His parents were Mary Farthing and Samuel Forsey. He made his way across the Atlantic to Newfoundland while still in his early 20s and roamed around parts of the south coast of the island before eventually settling down in Grand Bank. During this roaming he met an attractive young widow, Esther Petite Matcham, whom he married, probably in 1772. She was from Pass Island, near the entrance to Hermitage Bay, and given her birth name (Petite), it is likely that she was descended from some of the French settlers who had refused to leave the area in 1713.

Their marriage lasted about 30 years and produced a number of children before George, who, in addition to being a small-boat fisherman, also traded with neighbouring communities and served as a sort of mailman for the area, was mysteriously decapitated while travelling overland to Burin in 1803. Esther lived to the ripe old age of 76, her headstone in the Old Methodist (Fraser Hall) Cemetery indicating that she died on July 19, 1827, at the age of 76.

The other George Forsey was from Symondsbury in Dorset, having been born there in 1745. He, his wife, Esther Hooper, whom he had married in 1766, their son Aaron, and possibly several other children, emigrated from England to Newfoundland in the 1790s, also settling at Grand Bank. It was there that Aaron Forsey met and fell in love with Elizabeth Forsey, daughter of the aforementioned George and Esther, and a dynasty was born.

Aaron, baptized on February 23, 1773, and Elizabeth, born around 1779, were married sometime in the mid to late 1790s. Aaron died less than a decade later (1805–06), leaving Elizabeth to raise their son, George Aaron, alone. Born in 1798, he married 15-year-old Amelia Gallop of Fortune on November 28, 1823, and they were the parents of ten children. In what can be viewed as a developing family trait for longevity, he lived to be 84, dying on March 17, 1883, and was buried, at his own insistence, in the long-unused cemetery on the north side of the brook, next to his father. His headstone can still be seen, a forlorn reminder of the many other early Grand Bankers who lie buried there in unmarked graves. Amelia, who had been born on July 8, 1808, died at the age of 57 on November 23, 1865.

Nicknames were common to differentiate people in small communities, many of whom had the same names. George Aaron Forsey was often referred to as "Black George": some alleged because of his thick black beard; others because of his temperament. His youngest son, John, also acquired a nickname; he was known as "Pointer John" after one of the ships he had built.

John Forsey, born December 3, 1838, was the fourth son and eighth child of George Aaron and Elizabeth Forsey. Born at a time when even a rudimentary education was a rarity in most parts of rural Newfoundland, he was able to avail of the limited schooling offered by various Methodist teachers who served the community in the 1840s and 1850s. An intelligent man, what he could not acquire formally he taught himself. This included shipbuilding and navigation and he excelled at both, constructing and mastering his own vessels: *Amelia*, *Pointer* and *Grand Master*.

His education was also sufficient to allow him to take an active role in the affairs of Grand Bank's Methodist Church, in which he was both lay reader and Sunday School teacher for many years, as well as officiating at baptisms and funerals if the need arose. He was also quite active in the Freemasons, having joined Lodge Victoria in Fortune shortly after its founding in 1871. Five years later, when Fidelity Lodge was chartered in Grand Bank, he transferred his membership from Lodge Victoria and became one of the most loyal and long-serving Masons ever to grace Fidelity Lodge. He applied his talents for leadership, fundraising and craftsmanship to the benefit of his lodge, serving on its building committee in 1905. He had played a similar role in the construction of a new Methodist school building in 1888.

It is little wonder, given his drive, his determination and his ability see his plans through to fruition that he won the heart of Christiana Buffet,[1] whom he married on December 15, 1863. Six children were born of that union; the oldest, John, died just three days before his first birthday, while the third, George Samuel, died at two years, eight months. The others were William, Amelia Jane, Sarah Maria and Leonard.[2] Christiana died on August 9, 1901, at the age of 64, while Pointer John lived to reach his 90th birthday, dying on July 14, 1929.

---

1. Christiana Buffett (October 14, 1837–August 9, 1901) was the daughter of Sarah Hollett (March 30, 1815–January 13, 1894) and William Buffett (October 11, 1807–January 21, 1894). Their residence was a large gable-roofed house located at 1 George Street, currently occupied by their great-great-grandson, also named William Buffett, and his family.
2. Christiana Buffett and John Forsey's children were John (September 23, 1864–September 20, 1865); William (June 28, 1866–August 21, 1936); George Samuel (April 2, 1868–November 19, 1870); Amelia Jane (May 9, 1871–February 8, 1937); Sarah Maria (January 5, 1874–August 25, 1972); Leonard (October 4, 1878–December 2, 1937).

Of the three younger children, Amelia married George Foote of Grand Bank. He was lost at sea only five months after their marriage when the vessel he was sailing aboard on a trip from St. John's to Grand Bank, the *Maggie Foote*, encountered gale-force winds and capsized off Cape Race in late August 1892. She never remarried and operated a boarding house, catering only to upstanding Methodists, for many years before her death in 1937. Her house is still standing and was the residence of Marjorie and Raymond French for many years after Amelia's death.

Sarah married Robert Dunford of Grand Bank, who was involved in the cod and lobster fisheries. They had three children: a daughter, Amelia, who married Howard Patten, the first formally trained pharmacist on the Burin Peninsula and, for many years, manager of his father's general trading business, J. B. Patten Sons; and sons Maxwell and Leonard. Sarah carried on the longevity trend, being only four and a half months shy of her 99th birthday when she died in 1972.

Leonard was a fisherman. He married Hannah Pardy and they were the parents of five children: John, Reuben, Irene, Sarah and William. Leonard, Hannah, Irene and William all fell victim to tuberculosis and died within a few years of each other in the mid-1930s.

William Forsey (1866–1936)

The oldest of John and Christiana's surviving children was William. Born on June 28, 1866, he attended the Methodist Academy in Grand Bank where he received a sound grade school education. In 1895, after a number of years of involvement in various aspects of the fishery, he and John B. Patten entered into a partnership to establish a general merchandise, fish and foreign trade business. This encompassed a retail outlet, situated on Church Street, and a number of ocean-going vessels, which were used to fish the Grand Banks for cod in the spring and summer and to transport the dried, salted cod to European markets in the fall. Ships in the Patten & Forsey fleet include the *Mary F. Hyde*,[3] *Edith Pardy*, *Theresa Maud*, *Dorothy Melita*[4] and *Flowerdew*.

Patten & Forsey was a very successful business venture, with expansion both in Grand Bank and to satellite operations in Lawn and Epworth. The house that William Forsey built on Church Street[5] in 1913 is testimony to the success of the business. A three-storey, gable-roofed dwelling, with a cross gable on the south side, and verandas off both the ground floor and second floor, it was an impressive residence, one of the grand early 20th century houses for which Grand Bank is well-known.

Following the dissolution of their partnership in 1922, both J. B. Patten and William Forsey formed new, competing mercantile establishments just a few feet away from each other on Water Street, near the rise that marks the eastern extremity of the land mass that gives Grand Bank its name. After a fire destroyed both their buildings on March 1, 1930, William Forsey rebuilt his premises farther west on Water Street, adjacent to Forward and Tibbo Ltd., which had been established by his wife's brother-in-law, Charles Forward, and his wife's brother, Felix Tibbo, in 1908.

In addition to his busy working life, William Forsey found time

---

3. Named for Pointer John Forsey's sister.
4. My grandfather, Thomas Bishop (Newfoundland Regiment #6076), was a crewman on the *Dorothy Melita* after the war. He liked the ship's name so much that he named his first child, my mother, Dorothy Melita.
5. This house still exists, although much changed on the outside. It is located at 32 Church Street.

to be involved in civic, church and social endeavours. He was a Justice of the Peace for many years and a member of the Harbour Board, which, beginning in the 1890s, embarked upon a systematic deepening of the harbour. For more than 20 years he served on the Methodist School Board for Grand Bank and was a driving force behind the building of a new school building in 1922. Like his father, he was a member of Fidelity Lodge, serving as its Worshipful Master on two occasions, 1899 and 1908.

Above all, William Forsey was a family man. He fell in love with a young woman he had known all his life, Sarah Forward Tibbo,[6] and the feeling was mutual. They were married on January 23, 1895, and their first-born, Curtis, appeared nine and a half months later on November 3, 1895. He was followed by Samuel Tibbo,[7] Christana Buffett, Frederick Chesley, Eleanor Louise, and lastly by twin boys, Gordon and Charles, who lived for just a few days after their birth on June 9, 1909.

All three of the boys worked in their father's business and inherited shares in it upon his death on August 21, 1936. Sam, who married Esther Stoodley of Grand Bank, sold his shares to Curt in 1942 and spent the remainder of his working life as a commercial traveller. Ches, who married Grace Francis of Grand Bank, was a master mariner. He also sold his shares in the business to Curt and acquired part-ownership in the *Administratrix*, a 427-ton coastal trader that was rammed by the Norwegian freighter *Novdal* off Cape Race on April 28, 1948, resulting in the

---

6. Sarah Forward Tibbo Forsey (September 20, 1871–July 23, 1944).
7. Sarah Tibbo and William Forsey's children were Curtis (November 3, 1895–October 20, 1993); Samuel Tibbo (May 25, 1898–July 5, 1979); Christana Buffett (June 1, 1901–October 10, 2006; Frederick Chesley (August 15, 1903–April 28, 1948); Eleanor Louise (June 12, 1906–February 25, 1986); Gordon and Charles (June 9, 1909).

loss of the vessel and the lives of Ches and four of the six crewmen[8] on board.

Both of William's daughters attended Mount Allison University. Eleanor went on to train as a registered nurse, receiving that designation from Simmons College, Boston, in 1930. She married Dr. Chester Harris of Grand Bank and lived most of her life in Marystown, where he had his practice. She died at St. John's on February 25, 1986; her remains were brought to Grand Bank for interment.

The other of William's daughters, Christiana, graduated from Mount Allison in 1922 with the degree Mistress of Liberal Arts. She returned to Grand Bank where two years later she married Horatio Sydney Oakley. Christiana was well blessed with the Forsey longevity gene. She lived to the age of 105 years, four months and ten days, dying in Halifax on October 10, 2006.

Curtis Forsey (1895–1993)

Anyone living in Grand Bank between 1965 and 1983 was familiar with the sight of a distinguished-looking, well-dressed elderly man who, daily, would leave his residence on Water Street, next to the Thorndyke, walk east along Water, cross the bottom of Church Street, go a few feet south on Church, then double back across that street to enter the post office. His return journey was the reverse of his outward one.

That man, as everyone knew, was Curtis Forsey. They also knew that he had not suddenly taken leave of his senses one February day

---

8. The four crewmen who were lost that night were Harvey Keating, Robert Lee, Arch Rose and George Welsh. The two who were rescued were George Barnes and Charles Fizzard.

in 1965 when he began taking this rather strange route to get to the post office. It was to avoid walking under the maple leaf, the new Canadian flag, which, after February 15, 1965, was hoisted each weekday to the top of the federal building flagpole near the corner of Church and Water. A man of strong principles, and unafraid to express them, Curt saw no need for Canada to abandon the Red Ensign in favour of the maple leaf (or any other flag), and he continued to fly the Union Jack from the staff on his front porch on Sundays and civic holidays up until he left Grand Bank in 1983.

These and many of the other principles that governed the way he lived his life were instilled in Curt Forsey from the day he was born. Even his name evinced the principles under which he was raised. He was named not for his father or grandfathers, as was often the practice with a first-born son, but for the Reverend Levi Curtis,[9] Methodist minister in Grand Bank at the time, who officiated at his baptism.

Curt's schooling took place at the Methodist Academy, where he would have come under the influence of such legendary teachers as Maria (Rye) Forsey, her brother Ray Forsey, Lionel Clarke, William Handrigan and Elias Hause (Hawes). From them he received not only the fundamentals of a grade-school education but also tried and true lessons on how to live life in a spirit of honesty, charity, camaraderie and perseverance, lessons he took to heart and practiced daily throughout his life.

---

9. Reverend Levi Curtis (1858–1942) served the Grand Bank charge of the Methodist Church from 1891 to 1894. In 1899 he became superintendent of Methodist schools in Newfoundland and in the 1920s was one of the founders of Memorial University College. His son, Pierson, who was born in Grand Bank, went on to become Newfoundland's Rhodes Scholar for 1912. He was the first of four Rhodes Scholars who had been born in Grand Bank. The others are Eugene Forsey (Quebec, 1926), William Rowe (Newfoundland, 1964) and Luke Pike (2007).

Upon completing the course of study at the Academy, in the late summer of 1912, Curt went to Sackville, New Brunswick, to attend Mount Allison College (its name was changed from College to University in 1913), the "Methodist" institution of higher learning that many young Grand Bankers had already attended and many others, including his two younger sisters, would attend in the years to come. One of his constant companions during his time there was Rogerson Lench, whose father, the Reverend Charles Lench, had taken over the Methodist charge at Grand Bank in 1912.

At Mount Allison, Curt enrolled in a business program, but did not complete a degree as work and war intervened. Some time early in 1915, after a Christmastime visit to Grand Bank, he and Rog travelled to the United States where Curt was employed in a metal manufactory in Waterbury, Connecticut, and later worked for a newspaper publishing company in New York City.

During his time working in the United States, he had ready access to news of the war in Europe and the plight of the Newfoundland Regiment, especially after its heavy losses at Beaumont Hamel on July 1, 1916, and at Monchy-le-Preux in April 1917. It was the United States entry into the war on April 2, 1917, that was the motivating factor in his decision to enlist, however; and, if he was to become part of this war, it would be as a member of the Newfoundland Regiment rather than the American Army. Rog Lench agreed.

After wrapping up affairs in New York, they left the United States for home on May 17, 1917. The journey took less than two weeks, as they made the whole trek from New York to St. John's by train, except for the few hours crossing the Cabot Strait on the ferry.

On May 30, 1917, Curtis Forsey enlisted in the Newfoundland Regiment, receiving regimental number 3828. The following day, one of his closest friends from Grand Bank, Jack Patten, who had been working for the Bank of Nova Scotia in St. John's, signed up, and on June 18, probably after visiting his family in Bonavista, where his father was now the incumbent Methodist clergyman, Rog Lench did likewise. All three of them were billeted at a boarding house operated by Mrs. William Blandford at 21 Spencer Street, St. John's.

After several months of training in St. John's, in August 1917, Curt was one of 350 or so new recruits who travelled to Halifax to join a troop and ammunition convoy en route to Great Britain. The Newfoundland Regiment, together with a large contingent of Canadians, travelled aboard the Allan liner *Grampian*, one of six ships in the convoy. Soon after their arrival in England, they were sent to Barry Camp on the east coast of Scotland, near Dundee, where the Regiment was undergoing training during the summer and early fall of 1917. In October the Regiment returned to Ayr, on the west coast of Scotland, where the training depot was set up at Russell Street School. He was there until the second week of January 1918, except for a two-week period at Troon, where he underwent special course training in bombing.

In mid-January 1918, Curt and his cohort were transferred to Hazeley Down Camp on the Salisbury Plain in the south of England before joining D Company of the Regiment in France in the first week of February.[10] At least he assumed he was in France, but the fighting was so concentrated in the area that he fought in both France and Belgium, moving back and forth from one country to the other without realizing that he was crossing an international border.

He spent the next eight months in France or Belgium, involved in fighting in the Third Battle of Ypres at Passchendaele

---

10. Since Curt's own account of his time in Scotland, England, France and Belgium is much more eloquent than any attempt I could make at telling it, I leave his letters to speak for themselves and provide only a bare summary of his war service.

Ridge in March and at Steenwerck, near Bailleul, in April. In May, the Regiment was ordered to report to the French city of Montreuil on the English Channel, headquarters of Field Marshall Sir Douglas Haig, Commander-in-Chief of British Forces in Europe, to provide guard duty. This assignment lasted until the middle of August, providing much needed rest and recuperation time, allowing the Regiment to return to strength before the final push.

By late September 1918, the Newfoundland Regiment was back in the thick of the fighting, part of the Allied strategy to drive the German armies out of Belgium and France and all the way back to the Rhine. On September 28 it travelled east from Ypres toward Keiberg, where it met the enemy at Keiberg Ridge, just north of the village. It was there that the Regiment once again showed its mettle, its members winning 12 major awards for bravery on the 29th alone. And it was there on the 29th that Curt was hit first on the right ankle with a piece of shrapnel, and then by two bullets that struck him in the left thigh, forcing him to find medical assistance and resulting in him being invalided back to England. Interestingly, even though he was struck in the thigh by two bullets, there was just one entry wound; there were two exit wounds, however, as the bullets did not continue to follow each other once they had made contact with his thigh.

Curt spent most of October at Bethnal Green Military Hospital in London, before being transferred to Bletchingley Castle Relief Hospital in Surrey, south of London. Bletchingley was not really a hospital but one of the many large English manor houses that had been converted to convalescent care facilities during the war. He was there when the Armistice was signed on November 11 and remained there until early December. He was quite overjoyed at not having to return to the fighting.

Following his release from Bletchingley, he was due leave, which he spent in London. On December 15 he returned to Hazeley Down Camp at Winchester, where he spent Christmas and the first few weeks of January 1919. His last letter home is dated January 13; he left England on board the SS *Corsican* bound for Newfoundland on the 23rd, arriving in St. John's on February 7. He immediately wired his father to let him know he would be home on the coastal boat *Glencoe* as soon as he could get there.

Once back in Grand Bank, there were celebrations marking his safe return. He had to travel to St. John's in the spring in order to complete the paperwork leading to his final discharge from the Regiment, which occurred on April 25, 1919. Then it was back to reality and the workforce. That work actually took him across the Burin Peninsula to Epworth, to Patten & Forsey's branch operation in that community, where he relocated on October 11.

Curt spent several years learning the management of the family business in Epworth. Living alone in a much smaller community than Grand Bank finally began to take its toll, however, and sometime in the fall or winter of 1921–1922 he put in motion a plan that he had probably had in the back of his mind for many years. He wrote to Hazel Tibbo, a young woman from Grand Bank whom he had known all his life, but who now was working in Halifax, and asked her to marry him.

It is highly likely that there had been some contact between them in the intervening years since they had last seen each other in Grand Bank. Curt never mentions her in any of his letters home from the war, but he often tells his parents that he has many other letters to write during his downtime, and some of these may have been to Hazel. In a letter to his mother in January 1918, he does "wonder if there was anyone belonging home got killed in the Hfx [Halifax] explosion." It is hard to believe that he was not aware that she was there attending the Halifax Ladies College at the time of the explosion.

Quite some years later, when recounting the story of the proposal, Hazel claimed she always knew that she would marry Curt Forsey. And marry him she did. After saying yes to his proposal, in the late winter of 1922 she travelled to St. John's via the SS *Sachem* where she and Curt were married by the Reverend Walter Bugden at Wesley Methodist Church manse on March 22. Rogerson Lench acted as best man, while Blanche Foote from Grand Bank was maid of honour.

Hazel accompanied Curt back to Epworth where they lived for the next four years. During that time, their first child, a daughter, Helen, was born on March 18, 1923, but Hazel made sure she was in Grand Bank in ample time for the birth to take place there. Their three other children (Jane on November 29, 1925; Amelia on September 28, 1928; and William on December 10, 1934) were all born in Grand Bank.

The same year that Curt and Hazel were married, his father and John B. Patten dissolved their business partnership. This was carried out without any evident rancour and a fair disbursement of the assets and was no doubt done with a view to the next generation of Forseys and Pattens. In addition to William Forsey's three sons, there were five Patten sons (a sixth, Eli, who had joined the Canadian Expeditionary Force in 1915, had died on September 1, 1916, from wounds inflicted by a German sniper some days earlier), and there was hardly room for all of them in Patten & Forsey.

William Forsey built a retail outlet on Water Street, while Patten built one just a few feet away. The branch at Epworth went to Forsey; that at Lawn to Patten. Forsey acquired his own deep-sea vessels; the first of these was the *Max Horton*, which had been built in Nova Scotia in 1918. While in Nova Scotia to purchase that ship, he made arrangements for the construction of another, the *Christie & Eleanor*, named for his two daughters. Launched at Shelburne in 1922, it, like the *Max Horton*, made regular trips to the Grand Banks, Nova Scotia, the Caribbean and Europe. During World War II it served as a transport ship running between St. John's and Halifax, and after the war it was used in the coastal trade. It sank off Indian Head, on Newfoundland's west coast, in 1946. The *Max Horton* had been abandoned at sea on March 28, 1926.

A third vessel in William Forsey's fleet was the *Helen Forsey*, named for his first grandchild. It, too, was built in Nova Scotia, at Lunenburg in 1929. Coincidentally, the *Helen Forsey* was launched on November 18, 1929, the same day the famous tidal wave hit the south coast of Newfoundland.

After a relatively uneventful dozen years as an ocean-going fishing and trading schooner, the *Helen Forsey* was involved in two remarkable incidents during 1942. The first of these was an astonishing rescue. On a return trip from the Caribbean in the spring of the year, some of the *Helen Forsey*'s crew noticed debris floating in the ocean some 1,000 miles south of Cape Race. The skipper, Captain John Ralph of Grand Bank, came round for a closer look and saw first debris, then lifeboats, on the horizon. Upon reaching the lifeboats he discovered 44 of the 47 crew of the 5,249-ton British ship *Loch Don*, which had been sunk on that morning, April 1, by a torpedo from the German U-boat *202*, claiming the lives of the three missing crew members. Captain Ralph, despite the tight quarters aboard the small schooner and very little food, took all 44 survivors on board and made for Burin, arriving there on April 7.

The vessel's second encounter with the destruction that could be caused by a German U-boat would not have anywhere near as happy an ending as the first. On September 6, 1942, on a return trip from Barbados with a load of molasses, the *Helen Forsey* was accosted by the German U-boat *514* off the coast of Bermuda. The submarine surfaced, ordered Captain Ralph to heave to and opened fire. Ralph immediately gave the order to abandon ship, but two of his crew, Arthur Bond of Frenchman's Cove and Leslie Rogers of Grand Bank, already lay dead on the deck. Ralph and his other crew members, Thomas Bolt, William Keating and Jacob Penwell, all of Grand Bank, survived the ordeal but spent 13 days rowing in an open lifeboat before arriving safely in Bermuda. The unarmed *Helen Forsey* went to the bottom of the Atlantic.

In the 20 years between the establishment of William Forsey Ltd. in 1922 and the sinking of its schooner the *Helen Forsey* in 1942, the firm underwent the normal growing pains associated with any fledgling commercial enterprise. Diminishing markets for salt cod fish in Europe in the aftermath of World War I led to the closure of the Epworth branch in 1926 and the permanent relocation of Curt and Hazel to Grand Bank. The Great Depression, which also had a drastic effect on foreign fish markets, resulted in lean times during the first half of the 1930s for all Grand Bank merchant houses. Then in 1936, William Forsey died, leaving the business in the capable hands of his three sons.

The following year William Forsey Ltd. was incorporated, with brothers Curt, Sam and Ches as the major shareholders. Both Sam and Ches had interests outside the business, Sam as a commercial traveller and Ches in the coasting trade; by the end of World War II both had sold their shares to Curt. In 1945 the corporate shareholders were Curt, Hazel and Philip Gilliard, who had become Curt's right-hand man in the business.

William Forsey Ltd. would operate for another ten years. With the loss of the *Helen Forsey*, the business was reduced to one schooner, the *Jean and Mona*. As trawlers and draggers gradually replaced banking schooners in the deep sea fishing industry, it became less and less profitable to send schooners to the banks. The construction of a fresh-frozen fish plant in Grand Bank in 1952 signalled the end of the once proud banking fleet that had made the town a leader in cod fishing in Newfoundland for more than 50 years.

It also signalled the end of William Forsey Ltd. In 1955, Curt decided to close the business, selling his stock to G. &. A. Buffett Ltd. Thirteen years later, on September 30, 1968, it underwent formal liquidation procedures and ceased to exist. The building still stands, however, having been used for various commercial enterprises in the intervening years, including an outlet for the Bank of Nova Scotia, a Handy Andy hardware store and a Steadman's franchise. Its current occupant is Sharon's Nook.

The advent of the Commission of Government in 1934 brought with it a concerted effort on the part of the new government to have the larger Newfoundland towns incorporate and assume at least partial responsibility for their own municipal services. It was 1942 before the first incorporated town, Windsor, came into being. It was soon followed by Corner Brook West. Grand Bank would be the third.

Municipal government did not come easily to Grand Bank, as many citizens were opposed to the idea, especially to the possibility of having to pay property and business taxes to cover the cost of municipal services and infrastructure such as the installation of water and sewer systems, street maintenance, firefighting and garbage collection. One of those in favour and who worked very hard to have Grand Bank become incorporated was Curt Forsey.

A driving force behind incorporation was Grand Bank Magistrate Herman W. Quinton, who convinced the Commission of Government that a petition signed by 189 residents of Grand Bank requesting the institution of a town council was expressing the will of the great majority of the citizens. A counter petition signed by 111 residents opposed to incorporation was given short shrift by Quinton, who informed the Commission that the persons signing this counter petition were those who would probably receive the greatest benefit from a town council. The Commission of Government was satisfied and set the wheels in motion to have the necessary legislation drawn up for incorporation. Curt was asked to serve as secretary to the committee that undertook that task. The act incorporating the new Town of Grand Bank received Royal assent on December 28, 1943.

The first town council was an appointed one consisting of six members. Although he would have been a popular choice for one of the six positions, Curt refused to accept appointment, as he was certain that there would be accusations that he had done so for his own personal gain and that of his business. If he was to serve, he would have to be elected by the people of the town.

That opportunity came on February 2, 1948. The first council's term of office was to last four years, after which three of its members would step down. Their seats would be filled through an election and the three newly elected councillors would join the other three appointed members for a four-year term that would last until 1952. Curt sought one of those seats, which he won handily. The other two successful candidates were Max Dunford and Fred Tessier. They joined Sam Stoodley, Philip Gilliard and Percival Hickman, the remaining three appointed members. At their first meeting, Curt was elected chairman of council, the equivalent of mayor, by his fellow councillors.[11] As such he was the first person to

---

11. Merrill Tibbo, who along with Clayton Camp and Robert Riggs were the three appointed members of council who stepped down in 1948, had been the first chairman of council, in effect the first mayor of Grand Bank.

serve as mayor who had been elected to council by the people of the town.

Even though the council had been in existence for four years when Curt became a member, there was still much to be done. A priority was firefighting, as there had been two major fires in recent memory, one which did extensive damage in the commercial district on Water Street in 1930 and another that destroyed seven houses on the Cove Road in 1940. The council was able to acquire one of several surplus fire trucks that had been made available to the Commission of Government by the American base at Fort Pepperrell in St. John's. Other initiatives begun or continued during the next few years were the installation of water and sewer lines, street lighting, and improvement to existing roadways.

Curt opted for just a single term on council. No sooner had his term ended when he was asked by Grand Bank Magistrate R. M. Sparks to assist him in preparing a report into the damage to fishing property caused by a number of early winter storms that wreaked havoc along the south coast, but particularly on Burin Peninsula and Placentia Bay communities, during November 1952. In response to the storm damage, the Provincial Government had established a series of Courts of Enquiry under the direction of area magistrates to investigate the losses sustained by fishermen and report their findings to government.

The following summer Curt returned to England for the first time since he had come home from the war in 1919. He was part of the official delegation of Newfoundland veterans invited to attend the coronation ceremonies for Queen Elizabeth II on June 2, 1953.

In addition to his civic pursuits, Curt also served as a Justice of the Peace for many years, which enabled him to play a formal role in the preparation of wills and other legal documents and the settlement of property disputes when asked to do so by the parties involved.

A man of a deeply personal religious faith, he seldom attended church except for the yearly service commemorating Armistice Day in November and the Watch Night service on New Year's Eve. Yet he was a long-time member of the United Church School Board and insisted that his children attend church services and Sunday School as he had done in his formative years. When Hazel and the children were at church on Sundays he listened to services at home via radio transmissions from Wesley United Church in St. John's or St. James United Church in Montreal.

He was never a social animal, avoiding gatherings such as weddings (he did not attend the weddings of any of his children or grandchildren) and church suppers, but encouraged visitors at home where he spent many hours talking with friends and strangers alike on subjects ranging from the early settlement of Grand Bank to the folly of Confederation with Canada.[12] The one social gathering that was sacrosanct and constant in his life, however, was his nightly foray to Billy Matthews' barbershop. Located next door to

---

12. In the late 1940s, when the debate over whether Newfoundland should become a province of Canada was raging, Curt voted no in the referenda, not so much an anti-Confederate, but because he believed that Newfoundland should retain its separate identity within the British Empire and Commonwealth. In preparation for the 35th anniversary of Confederation on March 31, 1984, Curt and Hazel, along with seven other residents of Agnes Pratt Home, were asked by the *Evening Telegram* how they would vote if a referendum were held on Confederation on that day. Seven, including Hazel and Curt, stated they would vote for Confederation, one was opposed and one undecided. Hazel was most enthusiastic in her response: "I'd vote for it. Why not? We are better off now than we ever were. Canada is a great country." Curt had certainly undergone an epiphany in the intervening years: "Well I'm for it of course. You don't think I would be fool enough to be against it. I was a Confederate before Joe Smallwood could spell the word."

William Forsey Ltd., the barber shop hosted an eclectic mixture of businessmen, ship captains and other locals, who gathered there to expound upon the current price of fish, the state of the world economy and the future of society. Solutions were offered but seldom acted upon and the debate continued for many years until Billy Matthews' death resulted in the loss of their forum. The head of the pier could not replace the warmth or camaraderie of the barbershop.

In tandem with his aversion to large gatherings, Curt was never much of a joiner. He did become a member of Fidelity Lodge in 1926, a move that meant he, his father and his grandfather were all members at the same time; he seldom attended meetings after attaining the third degree, although he paid his yearly dues and maintained his membership throughout his life. Another exception was the role he played in the formation of a branch of the Royal Canadian Legion in Grand Bank in the early 1950s. He was a prime mover behind the establishment of Branch 24 and became its first president when it held its inaugural meeting in 1952.

His favourite pastime was trout fishing, a passion he developed while a boy and one that continued well into his later life. It was not a pursuit restricted to Saturdays as he could often be seen headed for one of his favourite ponds, fishing rod in hand, after, or even during, work hours on a weekday. He was not averse to having someone accompany him on these expeditions but had no problem going alone, for as he once remarked to one of his daughters, he was always fortunate in that he quite enjoyed his own company. The trout he caught would often end up on the supper table of some widow who had no way to procure this treat herself.

Above all, Curt Forsey was a family man. He did not lavish affection but each of his four children knew that they were loved and cared for by a very special man. A strict disciplinarian, he tolerated no nonsense and abhorred unnecessary noise, which he brought to a quick end with a reminder that he had had his share of noise on the battlefields of Europe and was not willing to have it brought into his home. Nor did he like the word 'grandfather,' insisting that each of his grandchildren refer to him as 'Uncle Curt.'

His kindness and charity extended beyond his immediate family. Hazel's sister, Muriel, blind from birth, lived with them from the time they set up housekeeping in Epworth in 1922 until her death at the age of 90 in 1985. Known to all as Auntie Boo, she was an integral part of the Forsey family and became famous throughout the town for her knitting ability. She measured a person by touching them to determine the length of their arms and the girth of their torso and then produced a sweater that was a perfect fit every time.

Muriel was the only immediate family Hazel had in Grand Bank for most of her life. Hazel and Muriel were two of four daughters and three sons born to Jane Hickman and Wilson Tibbo of Grand Bank. Her other two sisters, Ruby Maud and Suzie, both died as infants, while her brother Norman died at age 12. Her brothers Leslie and Clarence moved to Halifax and Nahant, Massachusetts, respectively, when still young men.

A Christmas baby, Hazel was born on December 24, 1893. Her father, an experienced master mariner who owned and operated his own ships, was renowned for never having lost a vessel under his command. His death in 1912 at the relatively young age of 57 came as a shock to his family. His wife, Jane's, death just four years later, at age 61, brought about the permanent breakup of the family unit. Muriel had been in Halifax attending the School for the Blind since 1905, so Hazel decided that that was the place for her as well.

In Halifax, she enrolled in the Halifax Ladies College, where she embarked upon a course in business. While attending the college she lived at the YWCA. Celia Glass of the YWCA provided her with a character reference in which she described Hazel as a person of "irreproachable character, earnest, sincere and conscientious." Following her graduation from the college, which included a diploma in shorthand, in 1918, she went to work at the War Office in Halifax, where she proved herself a very capable and valued member of the staff.

Hazel chose an auspicious time to live in Halifax. On December 6, 1917, a collision involving the French merchant ship *Mont Blanc*, containing a cargo of munitions for the French government, collided with the empty Norwegian ship *Imo*. The subsequent explosion killed 1,500 people with another 500 dying from injuries in the days that followed. A further 9,000 recovered from injuries sustained that day, while property damage amounted to millions of dollars.

James Reid, one of Hazel's colleagues at the War Office, later wrote that he had known her since the time of the explosion, at which time she worked very hard in the relief efforts. Reid indicated in his letter that she had "proved herself worthy of special recognition." He also pointed out that she was no mere office machine but a woman with a mind of her own and the inclination to use it.

While much of her daily life after her marriage was devoted to making a home for herself, her husband, her sister and her four children, she found time to attempt to improve the lot of others less fortunate than she was. Every Saturday for many years she sent the children around with soup for the sick, especially those afflicted with tuberculosis, and she had a reputation as the best gruel maker in town. Her homemade cakes, cookies and candy were treats that caused many children to break the tenth commandment.

A staunch Methodist, later United Church of Canada, Hazel was involved in the various women's groups of the church in Grand Bank:

the Women's Missionary Society, the Women's Auxiliary and the Four Fold Group. The latter had a recreational adjunct and Hazel, despite the fact that she barely reached five feet in height, was an avid and accomplished member of one of the Four Fold's basketball teams. After her children were grown, she taught Sunday School and many young girls longed to be assigned to her class, as it meant a visit to her house at Christmas and on other special occasions.

Hazel's focus in life was first and foremost her family. She liked to spend time with her children, reading to them, taking them on long walks, teaching the girls her secrets for a successful marriage and a wholesome and happy life. She was a formidable Scrabble player and loved to play with anyone who had the courage to sit down with her for a game.

If she had one regret, it was living in a house that overlooked the landwash. The windows on the front of her house were constantly covered in salt spray blowing in from Fortune Bay. The salt permeated the ground around her house, eliminating any possibility of being able to spend time enjoying the variety of fragrances and colours and the tranquility that are provided by a garden of one's own.

The house where Curt and Hazel lived is still standing in Grand Bank. A three-storey gable-roofed house with a commanding view of Fortune Bay, it is located at 31 Water Street, just east of the Thorndyke. It had been Hazel's father's house, which William Forsey had bought several years before Curt and Hazel's marriage. It was almost as if he knew what the future would bring.

Even though their children had been long gone, Curt and Hazel remained in their own home until 1983 when Curt, age 87 at the time, broke his hip in a fall. He and Hazel, who was two years older than Curt, made the painful decision to move to the Agnes Pratt Home in St. John's. Hazel died there on June 16, 1987, at the age of 93. Curt lived on alone for another six years. His death came on October 20, 1993, just two weeks short of his 98th birthday. Both Hazel and Curt are buried in the United Church Cemetery in Grand Bank.

The family name Forsey is derived from the ancient Gaelic name "Fearsithe" meaning "man of peace." This is a most appropriate descriptor for Curt Forsey; that is what he was all his life: a man who made friends easily and cherished those friendships; a young soldier who went to war for the sake of peace; a family man who raised his children to respect themselves and others; a businessman who valued and encouraged good relations with his competitors and his customers; a fisherman who appreciated the peaceful and contemplative time an hour at a trout pond could provide; a man who added to the serenity and meaning of his own life by helping others; a man who was proud to call himself a Grand Banker and one whom all Grand Bankers can be equally proud in paying full and deserved homage to as one of their one.

> Bert Riggs
> St. John's, NL
> May 15, 2007

THE LETTERS

21 Spencer Street[1]
St. John's,
Nfld[2]

Dear Mother,

I received a letter from you a few days ago and was glad indeed to hear from you.

No doubt you have been waiting for a letter from me for quite awhile but we have been drilling[3] very hard and I have been sick and everything else but not serious. I didn't miss any drill hours. There were two nights I felt quite sick. There is one thing I wish you would attend to. I lent Sam[4] $10 to come home with. Could you

---

1. The residence of William J. Blandford, a carpenter, and his wife, who took in boarders. Curt's friend, John B. (Jack) Patten, had boarded there while working in St. John's prior to his enlistment, and it appears that Curt and Rogerson Lench were boarding there, too, and not at the Princess Rink on Factory Lane where most of the new recruits were billeted while undergoing preliminary training and waiting to be shipped overseas.
2. This letter is undated. The envelope it was sent in bears a postmark indicating that it was processed at the St. John's Post Office at 7:30 a.m., June 21, 1917. It was probably written the previous day.
3. Drilling or marching took place at the Parade Ground at Fort Townshend, site of the present-day headquarters of the Royal Newfoundland Constabulary, and at Fort William, present site of the Fairmont Newfoundland. Rifle practice took place at a rifle range on the Southside Road.
4. Samuel Tibbo Forsey (1898–1979), Curt's brother, second of Sarah Tibbo and William Forsey's seven children. After two years at Upper Canada Business College in Chatham, Ontario, he returned home to enter the family business, spending several years at the Patten & Forsey branch

send it to me as soon as possible, as I am not drawing my full pay, only 50 ¢ per day, and I have an extra suit of uniform I have to buy, as you have to have two and the regiment supplies only one and it will cost $33 so you see they don't give you any. Sam told me he'd see that I got it as soon as he got home but I haven't got it yet.

They have got me down to go by the next draft. I told them today that I wanted home leave first and they scratched it off, but I'm still not sure whether they will let us go or not. I hope they will though.

I saw Hettie[5] about a week ago and intended seeing her again but didn't. I was quite sick with inoculation and didn't go out.

Rog Lench[6] is here in uniform. Jack,[7] Lench & I am at the same house. Lench & I have a room together.

---

in Epworth. With the dissolution of the Patten & Forsey partnership in 1922 and the establishment of William Forsey Limited, he worked at the latter establishment. Following his father's death in 1936, Sam and his brothers, Curt and Ches, became partners in the business. Sam sold his shares to Curt in 1942 and spent the remainder of his working life as a commercial traveller. He married Esther Nicholle Stoodley (1904–1995) on October 12, 1932. They had one son, George Sydney Forsey.

5. Henrietta (Hettie) Tibbo Maddock (1887–1970), Curt's mother's sister, married Austin Maddock (1888–1959) of Carbonear on December 7, 1916. Their daughter Eleanor resides in St. John's. As Hettie was only ten years older than Curt, this may account for his use of her first name without the use of the prefix Aunt.

6. Corporal James Rogerson Lench (1898–1954), Newfoundland Regiment #3862, son of Emma Harris and the Reverend Charles Lench. It was during Charles Lench's four-year incumbency as Methodist minister at Grand Bank (1912–1916) that Curtis Forsey and Rog Lench met and became good friends. Rog was noted for his excellent vioce and was often called upon to perform in church choirs and public concerts, and especially in the Poppy Day and Forget-me-not radio broadcasts.

7. Private John (Jack) Benjamin Patten (1896–1981), Newfoundland Regiment #3831, was the son of Julia Lawrence (1868–1942) and George Patten (1864–1902) of Grand Bank. His father was a brother of

How is all the family? I suppose they are well though. I told Sam father had a horse to work this summer. You should have seen his mouth drop.

I am invited down to tea with Green, Perlin's[8] man, to-night to supper.

I wish you'd hurry up and send me the money as I'll need it in a few weeks and come to St. John's as soon as possible.

                    Your Loving Son
                            Curt

John B. Patten, Curt's father's partner in Patten & Forsey. At the time of his enlistment in April 1917, he was employed by the Bank of Nova Scotia in St. John's, boarding with the Blandfords at 21 Spencer Street. Following the war, he spent time in Grand Bank and Lawn working for Patten & Forsey and after 1922 for J. B. Patten Sons, before moving to New Bedford, Massachusetts, where he worked for the New Bedford Fishermen's Union. He married Blanche Edwards of Lawn at St. John's on September 3, 1929, and they had four children: John L., Susan, Muriel and George. He died at Fall River, Massachusetts, on June 25, 1981.

8. E. Mendel Greene (1890–19??) was born in Dublin, Ireland, of Jewish ancestry. He came to St. John's in 1912, where he went to work with I. F. Perlin and Company. By 1921 he was an accountant with that firm, and later became manager of Perlin's clothing factory on Henry Street. As Perlin operated a wholesale business and sold to outport merchants, it is quite likely that Greene may have begun work as a saleman and travelled the south coast circuit, where he would have met Curt and his father during sales visits to Grand Bank. They obviously knew each other well enough for Curt to be invited to supper at Greene's boarding house at 41 Queen's Road. By 1924 he was a Director of I. F. Perlin and Company, but shortly after that year he seems to have left Newfoundland.

21 Spencer Street
St. John's
July 29/17

Dear Father,

I wrote you a few days ago[9] this is Sunday. I thought I'd drop you another line & tell you that I expect to leave St. John's about Thursday, as far as we know on the "Florizel"[10] to Halifax, and from there across to Scotland.

Of course nobody knows when or how but I have heard this going and I am pretty sure I am going Thursday I was warned yesterday for overseas.

I took part of my examinations for Lance Corporal yesterday and will finish to-morrow.

Steve Smith[11] asked me to be his orderly while I was in

---

9. This statement would indicate that some of Curt's letters to his parents are missing, as this is the first extant letter after the one bearing the postmark June 21, 1917.
10. SS *Florizel* was a passenger and cargo ship belonging to Bowring Brothers Ltd., of St. John's. It took the First Five Hundred members of the Newfoundland Regiment to England in October 1914 and was used as a troop transport on several other occasions before it was wrecked near Renews on Newfoundland's Southern Shore on February 26, 1918, with the loss of 94 lives.
11. Second Lieutenant Stephen K. Smith (1894–1981), Newfoundland Regiment #931, was born in Harbour Breton, the son of Mary Hutchings and John Smith. Wounded at Beaumont Hamel and at Bailleul, he rose through the ranks and was eventually promoted to Second Lieutenant. After the war he spent two years as Newfoundland's Trade Commissioner

Scotland so if I do that I will have a much better time than if I didn't & have only to drill.

Capt. O'Grady[12] told some of us yesterday that we were going across on a big ship. The "Olympic"[13] is now in Halifax so we surmised that she was going to take us across.

I am wiring Mother to-morrow so as she will be over to see me away.[14]

I almost wish she wasn't around one way as I know she will find it hard, but I'm glad to think she can be here.

---

in Portugal (1921–1923) before becoming superintendent of fire and safety with the Newfoundland Power and Paper Company in Corner Brook (1925–1935). From 1956 to 1966 he was Liberal member of the House of Assembly for Port au Port. He died November 9, 1981. His brother, Samuel R. Smith (1889?–1917), Newfoundland Regiment #932, joined up on the same day. He was killed at Monchy on April 14, 1917.

12. Captain Jeremiah J. O'Grady (1880–1967), Newfoundland Regiment, was born in Charlottetown, Prince Edward Island, but his family moved to St. John's while he was still a small child. An officer in the Catholic Cadet Corps boys' brigade, he joined the Newfoundland Regiment soon after the outbreak of war and was subsequently commissioned first as Lieutenant and in 1916 as Captain. Following a period of training in England, he returned to St. John's where he was assigned duties as senior instructor of recruits. After the war, he taught physical training at St. Bonaventure's College and other Catholic schools in St. John's and also at Memorial University College.

13. RMS *Olympic*, launched on October 20, 1910, was the first of the Olympic-class ocean liners, which included the *Titanic* and the *Britannic*, built by the White Star Line to rival the largest ships in the Cunard fleet, the *Lusitania* and the *Mauretania*. It was brought into service as a troop carrier during World War I, travelling between Halifax and England, transporting Canadian and Newfoundland troops. The *Olympic* was attacked by the German submarine *U-103* on May 12, 1918. After avoiding the torpedo fired at it, it rammed and sank the submarine, the only known sinking of a warship of any kind by a merchant vessel during the war.

14. Sarah Tibbo Forsey, Curt's mother, was probably visiting Carbonear where her sisters Henrietta and Winifred, who had both married men from that place, lived. She could get to St. John's from there on the train in a few hours.

We have been having good weather lately, almost too hot for drill.

I have had a section of my own to drill for the last few days, so I think I can get ahead a little if I like.

Roy Grandy[15] is coming home with the next lot that come. I guess he will be glad to get back. I would like very much to see him before I went.

If we go over on the "Olympic" I guess I won't be sea sick as she is so large that we would hardly find any swell.

However I guess when you receive this I'll be on my way. I'll try and drop a line or card from Hfx [Halifax] and I'll wire you anyway when I leave for overseas.

When you write address me

    Private Curtis Forsey # 3828

    1st Nfld Regiment

    Where ever I am always put my number on the letter.

        I remain Your Son

        Curt

---

15. Captain Roy Stanley Grandy (1894–1965), Newfoundland Regiment #662. Born in Bay L'Argent, Grandy joined the Newfoundland Regiment in 1914 and went overseas. He transferred to the Royal Flying Corps in 1916 and was raised to the rank of Flight Commander before being discharged at the end of the war. He served as a flight instructor with the Canadian Air Force (1920–1922) and in the employ of Laurentide Air Services Limited (1922–1924), during which time he established the first Canadian airmail route.

Returing to Newfoundland in 1924, he worked as a seal spotter for a season before rejoining the Canadian Air Force in 1925. During World War II he was Commanding Officer at RCAF Station Torbay in St. John's. He retired from the Air Force at the end of the war and worked in private enterprise and for government (Newfoundland's Director of Civil Defence, 1952–1953) both in Newfoundland and in Nova Scotia before retiring to Toronto.

Halifax

Aug. 8/17

Dear Father,

We arrived here Monday from St. John's on the Florizel after a very pleasant trip and smooth water. We are hung up here for awhile. I expect to leave for Scotland to-morrow or the next day.

I got my Lance Corporal stripe before leaving St. John's. Mother sewed them on for me there.

All the boys from G. Bank are well. I saw Bob Janes[16] & Bert Riggs[17] last night. I'm going to try and see Mr. Courtney[18] & Hefferman.[19]

---

16. Robert Bond Janes (1892-19??) was the son of Avelina Bond and George Janes, and brother of Ursula Janes Squires. (See note 130.) He moved from Grand Bank before the outbreak of World War I. He served with the Canadian Expeditionary Force during the war, after which he lived in various parts of North America, returning to Grand Bank for occasional visits.
17. Bert Riggs (1891-1948) was the son of Eleanor Stoodley (1868-1951) and Benjamin George Riggs (1868-1938) of Grand Bank. He was working in Halifax at the time of this letter, but returned to Grand Bank shortly after the Halifax Explosion later that year, where he married Rosella Stoodley (1886-1961) on October 24, 1918, and raised two children: Grace (1919-1984) and Frank (1921-1996). Frank is the father of the editor of this volume.
18. Henry Hickman Courtney (1867-19??) was the son of Lydia Hickman and Robert Courtney of Grand Bank. He entered the fishery as a young age and eventually became a master mariner and dealer. His wife Dinah (1869-1900) died at the age of 31, leaving Henry to raise their only child, William George. Shortly after he died, on June 13, 1914, at the age of 17, Henry moved to Halifax.
19. Elihu Hefferman (1866-1918) was in partnership for many years with

Curtis Forsey

We are in Barracks now and I'm writing in my bed sack so you see we are at an inconvenience. The food is simply awful. Of course it's no use for us to kick. I can't eat it. I've taken my meals down town since I came here but my money is nearly gone so I have to eat here, and put up with it.

I am getting rather tired of this place now, & I wish we were on our way to Scotland.

Mother is bringing home a raincoat I bought in St. John's. I bought it before I left, paid $15 for it and found out I couldn't bring it, so I guess it will fit you all right, so if you like you can slip a $10 bill in the next letter you write not compulsory of course.

Well I guess I'll close now. Hoping this finds all the family well.

I was glad to hear John Thornhill[20] made a good trip again. The fall in has sounded so I'll have to stop.

from
Curt

Grand Bank native Henry Camp (1877–1955) in a carpentry business. As Hefferman is not a Grand Bank name, he probably moved there from some other part of Newfoundland. He certainly lived there from the late 1880s or early 1890s, as he was admitted to membership in Fidelity Masonic Lodge in Grand Bank on December 1, 1893, and was elected Worshipful Master of the Lodge in 1906. Given the scrutiny that accompanies an application for membership, he would have to have been living there long enough for the members to be convinced that he was a man of sterling character in order to admit him to their fraternity. He moved to Halifax sometime before 1917, as this letter indicates, and was killed there in a train accident on September 21, 1918, leaving a wife, two daughters, and one son.

20. Captain John Thornhill (1881–1947), captain of several Grand Bank deep-sea fishing schooners, including a number owned by Patten & Forsey and several he owned himself. His family home, the Thorndyke, was built in 1917 and has become a Grand Bank landmark.

P. S. The order was just given for us to get ready to embark aboard the transport.

CF

Barry Camp[21]
Scotland
Aug. 26/17

Dear Father,

We arrived here Friday morning 24th after quite an agreeable passage across. I wasn't troubled any with sickness.

We came in an Allan Liner[22] with over a thousand other Canadians which made 1500 altogether.

We are at present camping but expect to go back to Ayr[23] or

---

21. Barry is located in the Firth of Tay on the east coast of Scotland, near the city of Dundee. Despite strong objections from the Newfoundland Government, which was suspect of the reasons being given for the move, on July 3, 1917, the Newfoundland Regiment's 2nd Battalion was transferred to the Barry Links, a tent camp just outside the village of Barry, where it would undergo training for the remainder of the summer. The Regiment was returned to Ayr in early October, where it was quartered at the Russell Street School.
22. The Allan Line was founded in 1854 as the Montreal Ocean Steamship Company. It ran a weekly passenger and cargo service between Liverpool, England, and Quebec City from 1854 until 1917 and a number of other transatlantic voyages between British and North and South American destinations in the intervening years. The Montreal Ocean Steamship Company merged with Canadian Pacific in 1915, a fact not made public until two years later. A number of its ships (*Calgarian*, *Grampian*) served as troop transports during the war, carrying Canadian and Newfoundland soldiers to England.
23. Ayr, a town on the Firth of Clyde on the southwest coast of Scotland, was the location of the overseas depot of the Newfoundland Regiment from August 1915 to July 1917 and again from October 1917 to January 1918. The members of the Regiment developed a deep and abiding friendship with

somewhere else in a few weeks. The country is very nice, and the nearest place to the camp is about 2 miles and it is quite small. The city of Dundee[24] is nine miles from us.

We are camping now with a large number of Scots. I think a great number of them are conscripts.

I expect to go up to Edinburgh or some place in a few weeks time for a course in Bombing, Bayonet or Musketry. A Lance Corporal is not much. Of course its better than a private but if I do good at it I expect to get three of them (stripes) before I go to France.

The camping grounds are very poor here & I just as soon be in France.

A few nights before we got here they were flooded out as the ground here is below sea level.

We are not allowed to say what ship we came on. We were ten days coming and in company with 5 more including a cruiser. When we were about 300 miles off we were met by 6 British destroyers and escorted in. One night it blew quite hard but that was all. They feed us fairly good here. Of course nothing fancy & clean, but quite good, also on the ship.

But in Halifax what they gave us wasn't fit for pigs. I used to go down and it used to almost turn my stomach and I'd have to leave.

---

the citizens of Ayr. A number of men from Ayr joined the Newfoundland Regiment and a number of members of the Regiment married women from there. The affection the Newfoundlanders had for Ayr was demonstrated by the members of the 1st Battalion who were granted travel leave after returning from France in late April 1919. Of the 125 travel warrants applied for, 73 (58.4%) were for Ayr, with another 22 for Glasgow and 19 for Edinburgh.

24. Dundee is situated on the northern side of the entrance of the Firth of Tay on the east side of Scotland. In the summer of 1917, this city of 166,000 was a common destination for members of the Newfoundland Regiment, stationed just a few miles away at the Barry Links.

Curtis Forsey

I took nearly all my meals out and got broke and they only gave us a pound when we arrived.

I have dreamt of sitting down to a good meal once since I came here and when I woke up in the morning I was a little disappointed. We sleep on the bare board and have 3 blankets. I cannot imagine a man taking soldiering as a profession except having a commission, & these things are hard to get, but if I come through and can get one, I think I'd like it all right.

I guess I'd better close. Don't forget to put my regimental number 3828 on my letters when addressing my mail, and also D company.

Your affectionate son
Curt.

Barry Camp
Scotland
Sept. 7/17

Dear Mother,

I wrote you a letter over a week ago just after our arrival here. I haven't received any mail since coming here. I received a letter from a Waterbury[25] friend that was sent to Grand Bank and forwarded on and was surprised at not hearing from any of you. I have just come off guard. Tuff[26] was Sergeant and I was Corporal of the guard for the last 24 hours & I feel nearly all in & I think he does

---

25. Waterbury is a city in Connecticut where Curt, after completing bookkeeping and accounting courses at Mount Alison University, Sackville, New Brunswick, worked as a clerk in a metalworks foundry for a short period before enlisting in the Newfoundland Regiment.

26. Sergeant George Beverley Tuff (1881–1963), Newfoundland Regiment #2, was the son of Margaret Wiltshire Turner and George Tuff of Old Perlican. Tuff was a clerk at the Royal Stores in St. John's when he enlisted on September 2, 1914, served with the Regiment in Gallipoli and at Beaumont Hamel where he was wounded on July 1, 1916. He was made Lance Corporal on November 6, 1916, Corporal on April 27, 1918, and Sergeant on February 12, 1919. At the time Curt wrote this letter, Tuff was acting Sergeant. He was demobilized on June 29, 1919. He later settled in Corner Brook, where he married Cerral L. Fillatre, and where he died is buried in St. Mary's Cemetery in Curling.

Curt's letter implies a connection between Tuff and Grand Bank: given that they "were talking quite a long while about Grand Bank last night," it would seem that Tuff spent some length of time there rather than a short visit. The reference to Aunt Mellie, who kept a boarding house, may mean that Tuff had lived at her house while there.

too. We were talking quite a long while about Grand Bank last night. He is about the same. Tell Aunt Mellie[27] he was asking for her.

Geo Tibbo[28] was here also. I don't know whether I told you before or not.

This is not a very interesting place, only camping ground. The nearest town is nearly two miles. Where I'm writing this is in a soldiers home in the camping grounds. It is packed with Scots & Nflders. Jack and I are here writing now. I guess nearly if not all my letters will be in pencil as a soldier can't very well have pen & ink, as it is so unhandy. I know a letter seems better in ink, but I'm only a soldier now.

We expect to leave here Monday or sometime next week for somewhere else. I think it will be Ayr, so I guess the next time you write you can address it to there.

I will be glad when we get clear of this as its very rainy here and after a big flood we are nearly flooded away. We had to get up one morning and dig trenches around the tents to drain off the water.

Still I don't mind it. I can put up with a lot worse, if it wasn't for the food. For tea we get sometimes a slice of bread about one inch thick, a mug of tea, then you have to go out and buy the rest.

I am enclosing a card of the grounds here.

With love to all the family I remain Your loving Son,

Curt

---

27. Amelia Jane Forsey Foote (1871-1937), Curt's father's sister, the oldest daughter and fourth of six children of Christiana Buffett and John Forsey. She married George Foote, who was drowned at sea, along with all hands aboard the *Maggie Foote*, in August 1892.

28. Corporal George P. Tibbo (1886-1961), Newfoundland Regiment #634. The son of Hannah Grandy and Samuel Tibbo of Grand Bank (see note 125), he did not return to Newfoundland after the war, spending the remainder of his life in Scotland.

Barry Camp
Scotland
Sept. 18/14[29]
Tuesday

Dear Father,

Here it is past the middle of September & still no letter from home. We are still here although we expected to be clear of here by this time but I guess we will be here till the end of the month. I think it's Mother's birthday Thursday isn't it.

I had my name taken to go up to Edinburgh for a course but they didn't send me. They took about 12 names but only 4 is going. I expect to go up with the next lot. If they don't I'll give them back the one stripe I have. If that's all they intend to give me they can keep that. I asked to go up on this course through Steve Smith but I guess it didn't work.

Well Barry is certainly an awful place, nothing here at all only one big field.

Jack & I went up to the city of Dundee Satdy [Saturday] night. It's quite a large city. You have heard I imagine of the Tay Bridge where they had the big disaster. Well that's where it is. Of course they have another now. Dundee is on the River "Tay". It's quite cold camping now & I am eager to get clear of it.

Say father could you send me some Edgeworth[30] tobacco and

---

29. Actually 1917.
30. A brand of pipe tobacco made by Larus & Brother Co., Richmond, Virginia.

some good chewing. You can get plenty of cigarettes here but I prefer not to smoke them, and chewing tobacco comes in find [fine] when route marching. I didn't bring any tobacco with me. The Imperial Tobacco[31] gave us a 100 cigarettes each but they are all gone, so I'd be very thankful if you'd send me a couple of lbs of Edgeworth or Beacon Hill[32] and as many lbs as you like of chewing. I know it's not clean but I'm a soldier now, and you get to have what you can catch.

This is very poor writing. I am writing this on my plate stuck against the tent pole. Grub is not very good here now. Sometimes we strikes a very good feed for dinner, but for breakfast & supper its nothing. Tonight for supper we only had a slice of bread & a mug of tea.

They only pay us 17 shillings a week, and that's not enough to

---

31. A tobacco manufactory, established on Flavin Street, St. John's, in 1903. It employed more than 100 people and produced several brands of cigarettes and chewing tobacco, including Mayo, made famous by Private Francis Thomas Lind (1879–1916), Newfoundland Regiment #541. Lind acquired celebrity status and the nickname "Mayo" from his letter home from Stob's Camp, Scotland, on May 20, 1915, subsequently published in the St. John's *Daily News*, in which he remarked that "The hardest problem we (smokers) have to face is the tobacco, it is almost impossible to get good tobacco in this country, a stick of 'Mayo' is indeed a luxury." This resulted in six separate campaigns between then and the end of the war to raise money through public subscription to buy chewing tobacco and cigarettes from the Imperial Tobacco Company, who supplied them at cost, to send to the Newfoundland troops. More than $8,000 was raised and many thousands of pounds of chewing tobacco and hundreds of thousands of cigarettes were dispatched.

In 1924, in recognition of the Mayo Lind campaigns and the role it had played in the war effort, the staff of the Imperial Tobacco Company commissioned a bronze plaque as a tribute to the memory of those Newfoundlanders who died in the war. It was erected at the Beaumont-Hamel Newfoundland Memorial Park in France.

32. Another brand of tobacco.

pay for what I eat outside so I guess I'll soon be wiring to St. John's for money.

I guess by Xmas I'll be in France. At least that's what we were told when we came here first.

This is all the paper I have so I'll have to close.

    Your son,
    Curt

Barry Camp
Scotland
Sept. 27/17

Dear Mother,

Well another week has passed and still there is no news from home.

Jack hasn't heard either so I suppose the mails must have got disconnected. As long as he doesn't hear, I don't mind as much.

We are still here but we expect to move up to Ayr on Tuesday October 2nd. It is getting quite cold now under canvas. I think it is cooler now than it is home this time of the year.

How is Roy Grandy. I suppose he is alright now he has done his bit, and his neck is safe.

We are drilling quite hard now especially with the bayonet. They seem to say that the bayonet is going to finish the war, so they are certainly giving it to us in good shape.

Tell father to please not to forget to send me the tobacco I wrote of last week, as its hard to get any good over here. The food is very poor indeed and very scarce, no sugar scarcely at all.

Jack & I went into a restaurant a few nights ago to get a meal & we ordered 3 eggs fried each. The waitress said that she would only give us two as she wasn't allowed to give us any more.

Sam Hollett[33] just passed along & said he would like to be

---

33. Private Samuel Hollett (1895–1964), Newfoundland Regiment #3877, from Grand Bank. It is apparant from the "settle up" reference in this letter

going into Father's office to settle up. I guess he's broke & hungry, & I tell you its hard. Last week I got broke Thursday & I didn't get my pay till Saturday. Thursday night I went to bed hungry enough and the same Friday night.

After I finish every meal I go over to the canteen and finish on biscuits and lemonade.

I'm expecting a five or perhaps more in the first letter I get from home for my raincoat, and if I get it, it will certainly come in handy as I only have 17 shillings coming to me a week after my allotment is taken out.

We are having good weather, but for the cold & wind. As we are right on the edge of the North Sea the wind is very cold indeed.

The ship we came over on was the "Grampian".[34] There were 5 more with us on the way. The "Celtic",[35] she had ammunition, "Tasconia"[36] & "Nascopie"[37] had Americans, "Calgarian"[38] escort. I

---

that he had been a crew member on one of Patten & Forsey's schooners. Some time after the war he settled in Hermitage; he died there on September 21, 1964.

34. Built for the Canadian-based Allan Line, the *Grampian*, an ocean liner with accommodation for 700 passengers, was launched in Glasgow, Scotland, on July 25, 1907. In December 1914 it made its first transatlantic voyage as a troop carrier when it transported part of the Canadian Expeditionary Force across the Atlantic to England. On July 9, 1919, it hit an iceberg just 45 miles south of St. John's. It sustained severe damage but remained afloat and under its own power was able to steam into St. John's, where it underwent repairs at the drydock. Only two crewmen, of the more than 1,000 passengers and crew aboard the ship, lost their lives.

35. There are three vessels bearing the name *Celtic* in the Mercantile Navy List for the war years. It is most likely that the one referred to here is the 680-foot steel-hulled *Celtic* built in Belfast, Ireland, and registered in 1901 in Liverpool, England. In 1914 it was owned by the Oceanic Steam Navigation Company Limited, 30 James Street, Liverpool.

36. Actually the *Tuscania*, built by A. Stephen & Sons of Glasgow, Scotland, for the Anchor Line of Glasgow. It was launched on September 3, 1914 and

forgot the other one's name. I heard that the Grampian was torpedoed on her return voyage. I don't know whether its correct or not.

Please don't forget to send me the smokes and also the chewing as everybody chews in the Army.

Remember me to all the friends and relations & love to all the family.

Your Son,
Curt

---

went into operation as a transatlantic passenger and cargo vessel early in 1915, in partnership with the Canadian-based Cunard Line, with a Glasgow–Liverpool–New York run. In September 1916 it was commissioned as troop carrier transporting Canadian soldiers from Halifax to Liverpool. In the convoy Curt refers to in this letter, on board were 1,236 men from the 16th Regiment of US Engineers travelling from New York to Liverpool. On January 24, 1918, while ferrying 2,013 American troops and 384 crew to Le Havre, France, the *Tuscania* was hit by a torpedo from the German submarine *U-77*. It remained afloat for several hours, allowing most of those aboard to get into lifeboats or other ships in the convoy, but eventually sank, with the loss of 230 lives.

37. The *Nascopie*, built in Newcastle, England, for the Hudson's Bay Company (51% ownership) and Job Brothers Limited of St. John's (49%), was launched on December 7, 1911. It was used in the Newfoundland seal hunt and as a supply ship for Hudson's Bay Company posts in the Canadian Arctic. The *Nascopie* was lost in a storm off Cape Dorset, Baffin Island, on June 21, 1947.

38. The *Calgarian* was the last of the transatlantic passenger liners built for the Allan Line. Launched in April 1913 in Glasgow, it made its first voyage across the Atlantic, from England to Canada, in May 1914. With the outbreak of the war in August, the *Calgarian* was converted to an armed merchant cruiser, in which capacity it served until March 1, 1918, when it was hit and sunk by a torpedo from the German submarine *U-19*, with the loss of 49 lives. In addition to its service as an armed merchant cruiser, it occasionally transported troops and passengers to and from Europe.

Ayr, Scotland
Russell St. School[39]
October 22nd/17

Dear Mother,

I received yours & father's letter yesterday and was very pleased indeed to hear from home again. The letters were just as a month on the way, so you see it takes quite a long time for letters to come here.

We are getting quite cold weather here now. I think it is much colder than we have it at home at this time.

I was glad indeed to hear of the schooners getting back safely from across. It is certainly lucky that none of them have been torpedoed.[40]

There were another draft of 50 men came here a few days ago from St. John's. They are putting the drill right to us now. I heard yesterday that we were due in France in six weeks time. I don't know how true it is still I hardly imagine that they would send us so early, but they seem to say that this is a good company.

The regiment had quite a cutting up a week ago in France.[41] Gray Bennett[42] was wounded I think but not very serious.

---

39. Russell Street School was a school building in Ayr that was turned over to the Newfoundland Regiment as its depot after it returned to Ayr from Barry in October 1917.

40. A reference to the Grand Bank schooners that had crossed the Atlantic to southern European ports with their cargos of salt cod that fall and returned safely home.

41. This refers to the Newfoundland Regiment's losses at Broembeek on

Curtis Forsey

Joe Evans[43] left here last week for home I think he is getting his discharge. He told me he was gassed.

Jack heard from home also & he says Roy Grandy had a great reception when he arrived home. I don't expect he will be good for much after this. If I can get out of it as easy as that I won't mind, of course.

Rain is about all you can get here now. Everyday it rains for sometimes two or three hours. If you go out you can never be sure of coming home dry.

I was sorry that you didn't get my coat when you went. Of course you can get it any time from St. John's. I guess I'll close now as I have some more mail to write.

I remain Your Son,
Curtis

October 9-11, 1917, in which 67 men were killed and 127 wounded: the Battle Honour "Poelcappelle" was awarded to the Regiment.
42. Private George Graham Bennett (1896-1964), Newfoundland Regiment #2888, the son of George Bennett, a member of the Newfoundland Constabulary, who was stationed at Grand Bank from 1902 to 1916. At the time of his enlistment Graham was a clerk with the Bank of Nova Scotia in Grand Bank. After his war service he re-entered the employ of the Bank of Nova Scotia.
43. Private Joseph Evans (1897-1975), Newfoundland Regiment #2793, was the son of Ellen Hepditch of Lamaline and William Evans of Grand Bank. He returned to Grand Bank after discharge, where he joined the Fidelity Masonic Lodge on March 12, 1920.

Russell Street School
Oct. 26/17

Dear Mother,

I received yours and father's letter a few days ago and was glad to hear from home again. I also heard from Sam to-day. He seems to like where he is all right.

I am doing guard again to-night, so I'm taking the time to do this now.

Ayr is not so bad a place altogether, quite a dirty and rainy town but I can very well put up with it.

I wonder will Sam join up in Canada when he is there. If I was he I wouldn't because he is quite small & I think he'd find it hard to put up with it.

We were on a 12 mile route march night before last. We left barracks 2 in the afternoon and halted at 6 o'clock, had our supper which consisted of a slice of bread and a cup of cold tea, then we got ready for a sham battle, that lasted about 2 hours and there was some firing going ahead for a while. We used bombs & machine guns & our rifles. Then we started to come back and got back at 12, and didn't it rain. It rained nearly all the time we were out.

Rog & Jack are quite well. Rog is gone down to the Isle of Wight[44] to see Bert[45] for awhile. I don't think he will be gone anymore than ten days.

---

44. The Isle of Wight is an island off the south coast of England, near Portsmouth and Southhampton.
45. Sergeant William Herbert Lench (1895–1938), Newfoundland Regiment

Curtis Forsey

We do quite a lot of route marching here now twice a week we one [?]. I hope you won't forget to send me the tobacco I wrote for some time ago.

I suppose everything is a bit fixed up for the year around home now. There are certainly some fish to be sent this way next spring. I wish they would send some this way as what we get here is simply rotten.

I guess I'd better close now as news is rather scarce and I have a few more to write.

I remain Your Son,
Curt

#1122. He was Rogerson Lench's older brother. A native of Greenspond, Bert Lench was working at the Bank of Nova Scotia branch at Twillingate before his enlistment. He saw active service at Gallipoli and on the Western Front, but was removed from active service after a gas attack at Monchy le Preux in June 1917 and the subsequent discovery of tuberculosis on one of his lungs. He was sent to the Royal Hospital at Ventnor, Isle of Wight, for treatment. Invalided home in June 1918, he lived for a time in California, where he founded and edited *Pegasus*, a poetry magazine, and was involved in writers' groups in Los Angeles and in New York City. He eventually moved to England, where he died at Belmont, Surrey, at the age of 42, from complications brought on by tuberculosis.

Russell St School
Ayr, Scotland
November 4/17

Dear Father,

I received yours & Mother's letters last week, was pretty glad to hear you were all well.

I also received a bundle of papers this morning. I heard from Mr. Hildebrand[46] yesterday in a reply to a letter I wrote John and as John is away he opened the letter and answered himself.

I am going away from here for 2 weeks on a bombing course. I am not very anxious about it as I would prefer a machine gun course to it but it came out on orders and I suppose I got to go.

This is Sunday and as I'm leaving tomorrow morning I haven't got anything ready yet, as my rifle has to be spotless and also my kit. So I got to get to work this afternoon and get it ready.

The place I'm going is called Troon.[47] It's only half an hour's ride from here and the course will only last two weeks so by the time you get this I'll be finished.

I wrote you some time ago about wiring me some money. £6. I asked. I haven't got it yet, still I should think you would have the

---

46. Mr. Hildebrand was Curt's employer when he worked in New York prior to his enlistment in the Newfoundland Regiment. John is probably his son.
47. Troon is a town situated on the Firth of Clyde on the west coast of Scotland, about eight miles north of Ayr. Soldiers were sent there for short periods of training at the School of Trench Warfare and Instruction in Hand Grenades.

Curtis Forsey

letter by this time. I was afraid it got torpedoed. I am very anxious to get it as I have to get another uniform, and some things and I [am] simply hung up waiting for it, and if I don't soon get it I have to wire.

I can't write a very long letter this time as I have a bit of work to do this afternoon, so I guess I [will] close. With best wishes to all the family,

I remain your Son,
Curt

Troon, Scotland
Nov. 13/17

Dear Father,

You can see by the heading that I am not at Ayr now.

I came up here the day after writing you last, on a course of bombing which is to last 16 days. I have 7 days of it over. I am much pleased with my results so far, but don't know how I will come out in an examination.

We start at 9 in the morning and dismiss at 4:30. Then it takes all night to write up your notes and drawings that you get during the day. We do all kinds of trench work here as well, as this place is specially adapted for bombing. I imagine they have a mile or more of trenches here. So to-morrow night we are going on a raid. I hope it turns out all right.

I don't know whether I'll get another stripe out of this affair or not. I suppose it all depends on what success I make.

There are about 65 NCO's of us here. I think I'm the only one that never had any bombing before, but I manage to keep up with them all right.

There are only 2 Nflds in the crowd. The other is a Seargent [sic]. I think he comes from St. John's.

I wired you Saturday for 6 pounds. I think you have that much left of the $100 I gave you all right. When I came to Ayr first I wrote and asked for it, but I don't suppose you got my letter, as surely you would have wired before this.

Troon is only 20 minutes ride from Ayr. I was over there and spent the week end last week and I expect to go down this week. I heard a few days ago Ned Nicholle[48] was killed.

By what I heard him & a Lieut. Goodyear[49] was killed together on a transport going up or coming back from the line.

I thought it was too bad as he had stuck it out so far, and not touched. I hardly know what time we will go out. I guess it won't be very long now.

I rather like this life. It's hard & you have to endure a lot, bad food and cold, but still there is something fascinating about it & if I could ever get a commission I don't know but what I wouldn't stick to it.

We got some good & hard training here at this school, everything is done on the run. I never thought I could do as much walking with full equipment as I can now. 10 miles don't seem

---

48. Company Quartermaster Sergeant Edward Henry Nicholle (1892–1917), Newfoundland Regiment #644, of Grand Bank, son of Hannah Jane Pardy and Philip Nicholle, died on October 10, 1917, from wounds received at Broembeek. A salesman before his enlistment, he was the only member of Fidelity Masonic Lodge in Grand Bank to be killed in the war. He is buried at Dozinghem Military Cemetery, Belgium.

49. Lieutenant Stanley Goodyear (1886–1917), Newfoundland Regiment #334, of Grand Falls, was killed at Broembeek on October 10, 1917. He was Transport Officer with the Regiment and he and Edward Nicholle were killed by the same shell.

All five of his brothers also fought in the war: Josiah, Roland, Kenneth and Raymond were members of the Newfoundland Regiment; Hedley, who was attending the University of Toronto, joined the Canadian Expeditionary Force. Ray, the youngest, was killed at Gueudecourt on October 12, 1916; Hedley was killed by a German sniper on August 22, 1918. The other three received various injuries but survived the war. Their story, and that of their sister Kate, who was undergoing nurse's training at St. Luke's Hospital in Ottawa during the war, is eloquently told by David Macfarlane in his book *The Danger Tree: Memory, War, and the Search for a Family's Past* (Toronto: Macfarlane Walter & Ross, 1991).

hardly anything now, if it's fine weather, but over here all you get is rain continually. I think when Lauder[50] called it bonnie, he must have been drunk, because the climate is far from lovely. For 3 weeks at a stretch it rained without any let up at all.

Sugar is certainly getting scarce here now. Us soldiers get scarcely any in our tea, in fact none at times. Butter over here is 60 & 65 ¢ per lb. Isn't it awful the price.

At the school here we get mostly bread & jam and tea.

We get a bed to sleep on here. That's more than we get in Ayr and to lay on a bed again was certainly good, as we sleep on the floor in barracks.

I got my boxes from home when I got down to Ayr Satdy [Saturday]. I needed the socks bad, and the cakes were fine, not crushed at all, but there was a small lot of tobacco that was the worst.

It's tea time now & I guess I'll close. Love to all the family.

I remain your loving Son,
Curtis

---

50. Sir Harry Lauder (1870–1950), Scottish comedian, who was knighted in 1919 in recognition of his entertainment of Allied troops in World War I.

D Company
Second Battalion
First NFLD Regiment
Nov. 25, 1917
Russell Street School, Ayr

Dear Mother:

I received my box of tobacco, and was very glad to hear from you.

I have received no letters since last writing.

I wired father two weeks ago yesterday for some money. I wrote him the day I arrived in Ayr & I have received no reply to either. I think I should have heard before this, so I guess he doesn't intend to send it at all.

Well I wouldn't want it only I want to get a decent suit of clothes to wear out evenings, as I am almost ashamed to go out with the other boys and they all have them.

We get 17 shillings a week and before Satdy [Saturday] I have it nearly all spent, so I guess I'll have to do without it.

I wonder sometimes if you get all my letters, as I write every week and I get one from home about every three weeks.

I got back from my bombing course all right. I did very well indeed and my officer told me he was quite pleased with my work. I made 75% on my examinations.

I half expect to get another stripe in the near future. I don't know whether it will come or not. If I do then I will be a Corporal.

No doubt by the time you get this you will have see[n] Clyde

Lake,[51] as I saw him the other day. I was going in the station to buy my ticket for Ayr, and who should I see but Clyde. Well I was thunderstruck as I wasn't expecting to see him at all. He was glad to see me & came down to the school to see us.

Well I guess by the time you get this it will be Xmas, and if you haven't sent me the money, I ask again to please send it. Don't mail it, but wire.

I think father has about $35 or $40 that I gave him, when I was home.

Well I guess I'll close now. By wishing you all Merry Xmas

I remain your Son,
Curt

---

51. Harold Bertram Clyde Lake (1884-1965), son of Edith M. Purchase and Philip E. Lake of Fortune; MHA for Burin (1924-1932); Minister of Marine and Fisheries (1928-1932); operated one of Newfoundland's largest fish exporting companies.

Russell St School
Ayr, Scotland
Dec. 2nd 17

Dear Father,

I haven't received any letters since writing last. This is Sunday night and I'm on guard, so I am writing.

We are getting quite cold weather here now. In fact I think much colder than home at this time of year.

I received a box from London today from the overseas club. Jack, Ren Riggs[52] & Sam Hollett also received one. I don't know whether it was the one you wrote me that you were sending or not.

There was a card enclosed with Miss. L. P. Harris,[53] Nfld on it. I don't know who that is I'm sure.

It contained a small plum pudding, 50 cigarettes, a tin of tripe, a tin of potted beef, a little bag of candy and a little bag of raisins & almonds, and a package of biscuits.

---

52. Sergeant Rennie Riggs (1895–1930), Newfoundland Regiment #3721, son of Mary Grace Lee (1861–1906) and John Riggs (1860–1953) of Grand Bank. He lived in Marystown after the war, but is buried in the United Church Cemetery in Grand Bank.

53. The actual identity of Miss L. P. Harris remains as elusive today as it did to Curt Forsey in 1917. One possibility, however, is that the card was actually signed Mrs. L. P. Harris, not Miss. If so, it may have been Lottie Pratt Harris, the Lottie being the shortened form of Charlotte, which is how Charlotte Pratt Harris (1884–1954), wife of George Harris (1879–1954), and a sister of the poet E. J. Pratt, was commonly known in Grand Bank. George Harris was a son of Mary Forsey and Samuel Harris. (See note 83.)

I had the plum pudding for dinner today. Some class - plum pudding in the army eh.

We are going to do our shooting on the range next week, and then I guess France will be our next move, & the quicker the better, and have it over with. Our boys had a big cutting up again last week[54] so I guess men are needed there all right. I hope we don't get there before Xmas. As far as I can here [sic] we will be going out about the middle of January. We get 6 or 8 days furlow before going there. So if money will allow me I will go down & see London and some of the cities.

I have not yet received the money I wired for. I hope you will wire it soon.

Max Clarke[55] is here now from Hospital. He didn't get much of a wound and I think he feels all right now.

The guard room is rather cold to-night as it is freezing out now and there is no heat on in here. You can certainly stand a lot when you have to. We did a 14 mile route march last week with our full pack and rifle. I guess it weighed about 70 pounds altogether. I managed to stick it all right.

I remain your son, Curt

---

54. This refers to the fighting at Masnières on Novemebr 20-22, 1917, in the opening days of the Battle of Cambrai, when 56 members of the Newfoundland Regiment were killed and 194 wounded, one of whom was 2nd Lieutenant Vincent Cluett of Belleoram, who died from his wounds a few days later in hospital.

55. Corporal George Max Clarke (1897-1918), Newfoundland Regiment #2973, was the son of Sarah W. and Lionel P. Clarke. He was born in Bonavista, but his parents moved to Grand Bank when he was still an infant. Max was employed as a clerk by the Bank of Nova Scotia in Bonavista at the time of his enlistment in the Regiment. He was killed by a sniper while transporting a wounded comrade at Poperinghe on April 18, 1918, and is buried at Bailleul Communal Cemetery Extension (Nord), France.

Dec 9/17
Ayr, Scotland

Dear Father,

I received Christie's[56] letter a few days ago and was very glad to hear from home again.

We are going to France on the 20 Dec. so by the time you get this I will be there, the whole company is going. The Battalion in France has had an awful cutting up recently[57] and there are only

---

56. Christana Buffett Forsey (1901–2006), Curt's sister, the third of Sarah Tibbo and William Forsey's seven children. After completing her schooling in Grand Bank, she attended Mount Allison University, graduating in 1922. She married Horatio Sidney Oakley at Grand Bank on June 18, 1924. They settled in Halifax, where they raised two children, Anne Forsey Oakley and William George Oakley. Christie, the last and longest-lived of Curt's siblings, died in Halifax on October 10, 2006, having celebrated her 105th birthday on June 1 of that year.

57. Cambrai, which is one of the Regiment's battle honours, was the battle that caused the prefix Royal to be affixed to the Newfoundland Regiment, the only instance of that happening during the war and only the third time it has been awarded to a regiment during wartime. The city of Cambrai is in northern France, about halfway between Beaumont Hamel and the Belgian border. Fighting began there on November 20, 1917, and lasted until December 6. In the first three days alone, 56 Newfoundlanders were killed and 194 wounded, dropping the strength of the regiment as a fighting force from 553 to 303. Eighty men were brought up from the reserve, bringing the numbers up to 383. Then came November 30, another day of heavy fighting: in the morning the Regiment's fighting strength amounted to nine officers and 380 men; by the end of the day one of the officers and 130 of the men had been killed or wounded. In just eleven days 281 members of the Regiment had been killed or wounded. It was an "awful cutting up" indeed and the prefix Royal was well-earned.

100 now there, so we are now going up to fill up the ranks. I guess we will also be soon cut up too as it's mostly open fighting now. I hope I get a good wound and get back to hospital for the winter. Still you never get what you want these days.

The weather is getting quite cold here now. We have to wear our great coats all the time.

We will be getting a week's leave before going to France. I thought to have some money before this to go but I suppose now I won't be able to go on it as you didn't send any to me. I often wonder whether you got my message that time or not. However I'm going to wire to St. John's and get it from my allotment. I never get a letter from you father. Why don't you write me sometimes.

                              Your Son
                                  Curt

Ayr,
Scotland
Dec. 14/17

Dear Father,

I received your letter yesterday of Nov. 1st and also Mother's of Nov. 17 to-day.

On your letter you said you cabled me £5 for a Xmas birthday present & Mother said on hers you cabled me £6 in response to my cablegram.

Well I'm sorry to say I have not received either one of these. If I had received my £5 I would surely not have cabled you for the £6.

On getting your letter yesterday, I at once wrote the London Joint[58] about it. But on Mother's letter she didn't say whether it was sent by the Bank or not, but I imagine it was.

All I am afraid of is that you didn't put my number on the cablegrams, because there is another C. Forsey[59] belong to Gambo. He

---

58. The London Joint Stock Bank was founded in that city in 1836. Joint-stock banks, which had originated in England in 1826, became quite popular because they offered to pay interest on both current and savings accounts, unlike private banks and the Bank of England, which only paid interest on any account in the most exceptional circumstances. Located on the west side of Prince Street, it was the bank used by the Newfoundland Regiment in London, and many of the members of the Regiment would have received money from home through that bank. In 1918 it was amalgamated with the Midland Bank, which, through acquisition and amalgamation of other banks, was becoming one of the largest banks in England. 59. Private Charles Forsey (1890–1952), Newfoundland Regiment #3651, of Gambo.

has been here all the time. He went to France a few weeks ago. I see now where he is back in hospital wounded, so if he got it by mistake I'll get it when he comes back.

I feel pretty bad about it as I have needed the money so bad and to think I didn't get it.

I am cabling you to-morrow to trace it, and I hope you will, without delay. I guess I'll be stuck for Xmas now with no money. If I do well I never had any better luck in my life and I suppose I never will. But if I find out this fellow has the money I'll put my bayonet as far into him that he will not need to go to hospital again. He'll never take any more money.

On my last letter I think I said we would be going to France about Xmas. Well I think that is changed now, as I don't expect we will go till nearly the last of January.

I trust you will fully look into this matter and follow it up, as £11 is too much to loose [sic], especially when anyone is in need of it like me.

Trust you succeed in finding it.

I remain Your Son,
Curt

Ayr, Scotland
Dec. 30/17

Dear Father,

I have not received any mail from home since writing last. They say that a Nfld mail was sunk. I imagine that some of my mail and also the parcels that mother was sending me went down.

I have got a trace on the money that was missing & received the £5 just before Xmas. I haven't got the six pounds yet but I have written the L. Joint concerning it and hope to get it in a short while.

We had a pretty good time here at Xmas. They gave us a turkey dinner in the barracks (some sort). The[y] had the place decorated all up.

The Governor[60] and Sir EP[61] was here about two weeks ago and paid us a visit.

There is talk of the Nfld Rgm. leaving here and going down to the South of England about 1st or 2nd week in January. I don't know if it is correct.

We should have been in France as they had us marked down to go Dec 20, but I guess we won't go until the middle or probably the last of January.

---

60. Sir Walter Edward Davidson (1859-1923), Governor of Newfoundland (1913-1917).
61. Sir Edward Patrick Morris (1859-1935), Prime Minister of Newfoundland (1909-1917). On January 1, 1918, two days after this letter was written, Morris was appointed to the British House of Lords.

I hope we won't go until spring as I imagine the trenches are none too warm now.

I guess Clyde Lake is home now as he was planning to get home by Christmas and I guess he has seen you and told you he saw me.

I shall be quite disappointed if I don't get my parcels as the scarf and gloves would be handy for me.

I guess I'll close now with wishing all the family a Happy New Year.

                        Your Son,
                            Curt

Ayr,
Scotland
Jan. 6/18

Dear Mother,

I received yours & father's letters a few days ago and was very glad to hear from home again, as it had been such a long time since hearing. I heard that there was a mail sunk on the way over, also a number of parcels. I wouldn't be surprised if a number of my letters and parcels went down.

I received the £5 father sent me in October about Xmas day. I wrote the London Joint Stock Bank about the £6 and they said they had not received it, so I guess there is quite a mix up about it.

Things are much the same around here now. The whole battalion is leaving here for the South of England. The Company I am in are not going as they intend to stay here until we go to France. I thought we were going in Dec. but we didn't. I hardly know now when we will go.

I wonder if there was anyone belonging home got killed in the Hfx [Halifax] explosion. I have been wondering whether any of our schooners were there at the time.

I am going to get a few pictures taken in a week or so. I will send them home as soon as I can get them.

I really know of nothing to write now, so I guess I [will] close for now as I have a few more to write.

I have not given up hope of the parcels yet but the chances

look slim of getting them now as it is so long since they were sent.

                                        Your loving Son,
                                                Curt

                              Hazeley Down Camp[62]
                              Winchester[63]
                              England
                                  Jan. 16/17[64]

Dear Father,

You can see by my address that I am shifted from Ayr.

They have shifted our depot down here altogether & it is certainly some place. We are on a huger camping ground and 4 miles from any town at all.

As far as I can understand we are in an extension of Salisbury Plains.[65]

---

62. Hazeley Down Camp was located near the cathedral city of Winchester, in Hampshire in the south of England. In January 1918 it became the new home of the Newfoundland Regiment training facility. The camp consisted of well-constructed army huts and included a well-stocked canteen and a recreation hut. The Regiment continued to use the camp as a depot and later as living quarters, until the summer of 1919, when the Regiment was officially disbanded.

63. Winchester is an ancient cathedral city and the administrative centre for Hampshire County in the south of England, some four miles distant from Hazeley Down Camp.

64. While 17 is written on the letter, it is obvious that this was the result of the change of the year from 1917 to 1918, since Curt did not go to Hazeley Down Camp until the middle of January 1918.

65 Salisbury Plain, encompassing some 300 square miles, is part of the Southern England Chalk Formation, mainly concentrated within the County of Wiltshire. Its most famous landmark is Stonehenge. Guglielmo Marconi (1874–1937), who first demonstrated transatlantic wireless telegraphy from Signal Hill, St. John's, in 1901, carried out early experiments leading to that

We are two hrs ride from London, 12 miles from Southampton, so you see we are away South & its just as cold here as it was in Scotland. The mud is to your knees and the walking is desperate. This is a very chalky district and wherever you go you have to wade through mud. There are over 800 Nflders here and I imagine over 1000 Englishmen of the Garrison Artillery,[66] and its one town of huts.

The huts are made of corrugated galvanised iron, not extra warm with a slow combustion in the middle.

Thirty men are in each hut and at night its not so very cold.

We only arrived here yesterday morning so I haven't had a chance to get around to see the place, and to tell the truth I'm not anxious.

The officers & men are not at all in love with the place as its so dismal.

The Sergeant Major told us last night that our only hope of getting out of here was to go to town and start a fight with the policemen, and the English soldiers then would shift us for peace sake.

---

demonstration on Salisbury Plain. It was a major training centre for British Expeditionary Force troops during World War I. Coincidentally, it was the place where the First Five Hundred of the Newfoundland Regiment was first accommodated in England, and it would be the last. The members of the Regiment had no kind words for conditions there in 1914, and neither did those who were subjected to it in 1918.

66. The Royal Regiment of Artillery, or Royal Artillery (RA), as it is commonly known, first came into existence in England in 1722. On July 1, 1899, it was reorganized into three groups: the Royal Garrison Artillery was one of these groups and was given responsibility for coastal defence and siege and heavy batteries. During World War I it was responsible for the heavy, large-calibre guns and howitzers that were positioned just a short distance behind the front lines to provide maximum firepower and support to the foot soldiers.

Curtis Forsey

I suppose now home you have all started for the western shore again. I hope you do as good as last year.

We thought we'd be in France before this but I guess we will not be going for a while yet.

But the sooner we get away from this hole the better I'll like it. I guess I'll quit now as its time to go to bed.

                        I remain your son   Curt

Write # 3828 L/C C. Forsey
Hut # 37C
"D" Coy. 2/1st Nfld Regmt.
Hazeley Down Camp
Winchester
England

Hazeley Down Camp
Winchester
Jan 20/18

Dear Mother,

I wrote you a letter a few nights ago and yesterday I received a letter from Father, so this being Sunday I thought I'd drop a line.

I may say that I have received the £5 just before leaving Ayr, and to-day I met the Commanding Officer and he told me he had a Postal order for £6 so I guess it is the other amount.

This is certainly an awful place here and the mud is awful indeed. Our boots are continually covered with it and we have all stopped cleaning them. I think I told you a little of this place on my last letter but it is not getting any better.

We are about 3½ or 4 miles from any town, and the first night I was here a fellow from Codroy (he is a son of the man who married Mrs. Hall of Channel) thought we'd take a walk out and see it so we started. We left to come in at 8 o'clock. I[t] started to rain and we got soaked long before we got in. We got near enough to see the lights of the camp and then we lost our way and couldn't find the road in. We found the road at last and got in nearly 10 o'clock. I shall never forget it.

Winchester is a very ancient and historic town and the next time I go there I shall buy some post cards and I shall mail them to you.

In the camp here we have Portuguese,[67] and a regiment of

---

67. Portugal entered World War I on the side of the Allies in March 1916. At

Garrison artillery and the Nflders, then are about 350 of the Women's Army Auxiliary Corps.[68] I guess you have read of them.

It is certainly a huge camp. It looks like a town. All the quarters are huts made of Iron and a sort of beaver board inside. We have a little stove in the centre of the hut and we certainly keep that going good. It's the only thing over here that reminds me of Aunt Jane's[69] oven.

Father spoke on one of his letters about Jack had made some very good friends there and hope I did too. Well Lench took him there. I think they were friends of Bert's. Rog never offered to take me there so I never bothered butting in. If he didn't want to take me I never bothered. So Jack and he used to go there I think nearly every night. But I never missed anything only the money I used to lend Jack to go there.

I guess I'll close now.

        I remain Your Son,
         Curt

---

first its participation was limited to the war at sea, but in February 1917 it sent an army of 50,000 men to the Western Front. These soldiers first saw action in Flanders, Belgium, on June 17. More than 7,000 Portuguese soldiers were killed in the war.

68. The Women's Army Auxiliary Corps was a branch of the British Army that provided an opportunity for women to serve in non-combat positions during the last two years of World War I. More than 57,000 women enlisted in this branch of the service between January 1917 and November 1918.

69. Jane Stoodley Bond (1841–1919?), whose house was a familiar gathering place for Curt and his friends. (See note 131.)

Union Jack Club[70]
91A Waterloo Road,
London, S.E.1.
Jan. 30   1918

Dear Father,

You can see by the paper that I am in London. I am here now on 6 days leave before proceeding to the Front which I expect to do Monday Feb 4th.

This is certainly some nice town but I fancy New York better as its more modern and up to date, but for old and quaint things London is best of course.

We had an air raid here last night. I just got off a street car coming home about 10 o'clock when I heard a bang and then next thing I saw was women running half dressed with little children in their arms, screaching [sic]. I started to make myself scarce and ran into the subway to get under cover. It was certainly exciting for a while. Then as soon as the bombs began to pitch

---

70. The Union Jack Club was established in London in 1904, at the instigation of Ethel McCaul, a Royal Red Cross Nurse who had served in South Africa during the Boer War. Offically opened in 1907, it was intended as a residential club for the non-commissioned ranks of the British Armed Forces and their familes. Its facilities included sleeping accommodation for 300, as well as a bar, restaurant, library, and rooms for entertaining. It was used extensively during both world wars, although it did sustain damage from German bombs during World War II. In the 1970s, the 1904 structure was replaced by a new building on the same site, which was opened by Queen Elizabeth II on February 12, 1976.

our guns started and it was certainly some noise. The "all clear" sounded about 1:30 this morning and that was when I got in. I always said that I would like to be here on a raid, and I certainly did get one.

I could laugh last night for fun, but of course when you look at the other side of it, one should not laugh, but then its funny after all and I bet if Sam was here he'd have a good laugh over it.

This is quite a large building. I think every allied soldier in the British army is here writing home - Australians, New Zealanders, Nflders, Canadians, Scotch, Irish & English soldiers - they are all here writing, I suppose home.

There is a Canadian here now I was just talking to. He lost his leg in Belgium last spring. Jack Patten went up to Ayr to spend his leave, Lench went to Birmingham to see his father's people, and I took the advantage of coming to London. I always said I'd like to come here.

I'm going down this afternoon to see the town of London. I tried to get in Westminster Abbey[71] Sunday but I couldn't so I had to be content to stay outside and look.

I[t] would take a long time to do this city and six days is far too short, but you've got to put up with what you get in the army.

Well father I'll close now. I'll try and write Sunday if I get time but if I don't get a chance to write again I shall in France I hope.

---

71. Westminster Abbey, the Collegiate Church of St. Peter, Westminster, is a Gothic-style cathedral dating from the 13th century. It is located in Westminster, which is part of London. It is the traditional coronation and burial site for English kings and queens, as well as the burial or commemoration site for a host of British politicians, writers, artists, scientists, and others deemed worthy of the honour.

Grand Bank Soldier

Please excuse the poor writing as this is an awful pen I have.

With love to all the family

>I remain your Son,
>Curt.

France[72]

Feb. 5/18

Dear Father,

I wrote you last in London a few days ago, so you can see that I have made a move since.

I hardly know what and how to write as the censorship won't allow me to say anything so far as news is concerned. There is not much altogether to write.

The Channell[73] [sic] was rather rough in crossing but I didn't get sick although many of the boys were.

I am having the best of health, and think I can stick it fine, at least I have so far. We are not settled down yet, so it means a lot of walking but I guess I'll manage.

Tell Uncle Len[74] I received his letter OK and hope he does well this year with his trap.[75]

---

72. He was actually in Belgium and would be for much of the year. On February 3, 1918, the 88th Brigade, of which the Newfoundland Regiment formed a part, were moved to Brandhoek, in West Flanders, where they spent the next few days building one of five trenches that would run between Ypres and Poperinghe. They would remain there until the 12th when they were transported to Steenvoorde, where they enjoyed a week of rest and ceremony before heading out for Poperinghe on the 19th.
73. The English Channel separates England from France and Belgium.
74. Leonard Forsey (1878–1937), Curt's uncle, was the youngest of the six children of Christiana Buffett and John Forsey. He married Hannah Pardy (1879–1935) and they were the parents of John, Rueben, Irene, Sarah, and William. Irene, William, and both their parents fell victim to tuberculosis.
75. By the second decade of the 20th century, the cod trap, invented by

I guess its hardly [worth] while wishing you a good year as I suppose you people would have one anyway. Jack & Lench & Ren Riggs are here now.

Tell mother not to worry about me at all as I guess worrying won't help it any. I guess I am just as safe here as anywhere so there is really no cause to feel at all afraid.

The weather is quite fine here now and rather warm, at least it felt that way this morning when we tramped for a few miles.

I hardly know what address you can put on my mail when you write, but if you or mother every [sic] send another parcel just stick in a few plugs of Mayo's[76] tobacco as it comes in very handy for use.

When you write Sam tell him I haven't seen any of Joe Radder's[77] friends here yet. I guess I better quit now as this is all the paper I can use for now.

> I remain Your loving Son,
> Curt

Write # 3828 L/C C. Forsey
Royal Nfld Regmt
British Expeditionary Force
France

William H. Whiteley while fishing at Bonne Esperance, Labrador, in the late 1860s, was a common feature of the Newfoundland inshore cod fishery.
76. Mayo tobacco was a type of chewing tobacco manufactured by the Imperial Tobacco Company, St. John's.
77. Probably a friend of Sam's from Upper Canada Business College.

Somewhere in France
Feb. 11/18

Dear Mother,

I wrote Father a few days ago and as I have a little time to spare think I will write you a few lines.

We are not where we were last time I wrote as we have shifted since a few hundred miles, and now we are near enough to the front to fully convince one that there is a war on.

The weather is now quite warm indeed and quite fine here.

Max Clarke is here with us now as well. There were quite a number of G. Bank boys with us. They are all well and enjoying good health as well as myself.

I hardly know what to write you as there is no news and censorship is strict. Therefore I cannot say much but I suppose as long as you know I am well and having good health you don't care. I shall write every opportunity I get so don't get anxious about me at all. I guess I am just as safe out here as anywhere these days.

I was sorry I didn't get a chance to get any pictures taken before coming to France but I didn't get my money till late and then we left Ayr for Winchester and I really didn't have much of a chance, although I feel sorry now that I didn't because with a little effort I could have done so. But please God I will come back to Blighty[78] soon and then I sure will have some taken.

---

78. An English slang word for Great Britain or England, a corruption of the Hindustani word *bilayati*, which means 'foreign.' It became a popular and

Grand Bank Soldier

I suppose now you are having the general winter home now are you with lots of frost and snow, but you have one consolation that you can go asleep and not bother about any bombs dropping. But in London its different I tell you. I saw one there and it was certainly lively for a while, so after all you people have a lot to be thankful for.

I guess I'll quit now, with wishing you good luck and love to all the family.

I remain your loving Son
Curt

#3828
Royal Nfld Regmt
B.E.F.
France

---

sentimental term during World War I, expressing a desire to leave the trenches and return to England. A Blighty wound was one that was not serious enough to cause death or permanent injury, but did result in the victim having to leave the trenches, hopefully to England, for a period of recuperation.

B.E.F.
France
March 17/18

Dear Mother,

I received a letter from you yesterday and also one from Min Hyde[79] from Lamaline saying she was sending me a parcel, so I am going to write her soon and tell her I received her letter and thank her for it.

I wrote you last about two weeks ago, since then I have had no chance hardly since to write. So if a week or so may slip over without hearing do not get uneasy as there will be times that I won't be able to write for probably two or perhaps three weeks. I wrote Christie & Sam the day after I wrote you last but didn't get a chance to post them until yesterday. You will notice when you get them that they are pocket worn: but I guess they will go all right.

I am quite well Mother and having good health all the time. A few weeks ago I had a very bad cold and sore throat but it wore away after a while and I'm quite well again now.

Max Clarke & Jack are well, also Lench.

This is St. Patrick's Day and Sunday, although I hardly know it is Sunday as the days are no different and you loose [sic] track of everything.

---

79. Mary (Min) Forsey Hyde (1836–1920), sister of Curt's grandfather John Forsey (1838-1929), married Ambrose Hyde (1834–1889) at Grand Bank on December 14, 1860.

Pierre Coxworthy[80] is here also and I think he is well.

I wrote to Sam some days ago also and posted it yesterday with Christie's.

I hope you are all well home. I guess you are though I suppose Christie's back from Carbonear[81] by this time is she.

How is Ches.[82] I suppose he still has the asthma does he. It's a pity you can't get any remedy for it.

Eleanor[83] is well too I suppose is she.

---

80. Private Pierre Coxworthy (1895-1983), Newfoundland Regiment #1304, son of Margaret Hennebury (1860-1926) and Fred Coxworthy (1866-1932). His father, who was from Kingston, Ontario, operated a general retail establishment in Grand Bank around the turn of the century. He also had Grand Bank's first automobile. Pierre was born in St. Pierre, which may account for his name. His mother and his younger brother Frank (1899-1979), Newfoundland Regiment #1820, were living in St. John's when the war broke out, while Pierre was working in Bell Island.
81. Two of Sarah Tibbo Forsey's sisters, Winifred and Henrietta, lived in Carbonear, so Christie was probably visiting one of them.
82. Frederick Chesley Forsey (1903-1948), Curt's younger brother, was the fourth of Sarah Tibbo and William Forsey's seven children. A master mariner, he was at the helm of the *Administratrix*, a Grand Bank cargo vessel of 130 tons, when it was rammed by the freighter *Lodval* in dense fog off Cape Race on April 28, 1948. Forsey, along with four (Harvey Keating, Robert Lee, Arch Rose, George Welsh) of the other six crew members, lost their lives that night. The two survivors were George Barnes and Charles Fizzard. Ches married Grace Francis (1905-1993) of Grand Bank. They were the parents of two daughters, Eleanor and Mary Florence.
83. Eleanor Forsey Harris (1906-1986), Curt's youngest sister, was the fifth of Sarah Tibbo and William Forsey's seven children. She married Dr. Chester Harris (1887-1971), son of Mary Forsey (1850-1913) and Samuel Harris (1850-1926), who with his trip to the Grand Banks aboard his schooner *George C. Harris* in 1881, is claimed to have ushered in the modern bank fishery in Newfoundland. A graduate of Edinburgh University, Ches served two years in France and another in the

Curtis Forsey

I guess I'll close now Mother. I will be writing you again in a few days

Good-bye for now.

from your loving Son,
XX Curt

---

eastern Mediterranean with the Royal Army Medical Corps during the war. He returned to Newfoundland in 1924, where he established a medical practice in Marystown and later served as that community's first mayor (1951–1959). He and Eleanor were married on September 7, 1936. They had one son, Chester Samuel Harris.

B.E.F.
France
Mar 21/18

Dear Father,

I wrote mother about four days ago so while I have a little time to spare I'll drop you a few lines.

Well Dad I'm still alive and well Thank God. There was a time recently that I wouldn't have given 2 cents for it. Our trench was bombarded by artillery and there are four or five of us left that was there.

I got buried in and my knee skinned that was all I got. It didn't hurt, but the cries of the dying and wounded hurt me a lot more.

I can say that I got a good baptism from Fritz[84] any way.

John Patten and all the boys from home are quite well indeed, all sticking it fine.

I am having good health and I think it must be agreeing with me as some tell me I'm getting fat, but I can't see it at least I don't feel any heavier. I feel my feet at times especially after a long walk and I expect some day they will give out on me as they are flat.

How are all our people home, Grandfather[85] and Uncle Len and

---

84. A nickname for German soldiers.
85. John Forsey (1838–1929), Curt's paternal grandfather, was a son of Amelia Gallop (1806–1865) of Fortune and George Aaron Forsey (1799–1883) of Grand Bank. Known as 'Pointer John' to distinguish him from other John Forseys because one of his vessels was named *Pointer*, he was a boatbuilder and master mariner who built and operated his own

Curtis Forsey

family. I owe Uncle Len a letter and I guess it is time I answered it. However, I'll try and do so soon. Tell Grandfather to look out to himself and not haul too many caplin this spring.

The weather is quite warm now and no frost at all.

Tell mother not to worry about me I'm all right here just as safe as anywhere. I felt after that night that it was God's care and answered a prayer that saved me. I got beat about a lot but didn't get hurt. There was a little fellow Bobbitt[86] from Gaultois got killed quite near me.

I'm going to ask a favour of you now. I'm sure you won't though. Don't do as some people do - publish letters they get from their sons. I wouldn't have a letter of mine published for anything and don't tell everybody around town, especially Mrs. Patten[87] or any of those people as they might get excited about it.

---

vessels. He was a successful fishing captain and very respected leader in the town. In addition the *Pointer*, two other vessels that he built were the *Amelia* and the *Grand Master*, the latter reflecting his interest and membership in Fidelity Masonic Lodge. He married Christiana Buffett (1837–1901), daughter of Sarah Hollet and William Buffett of Grand Bank, on December 15, 1863, and they were the parents of six children: John (who died three days before his first birthday in 1865), William (Curt's father), George Samuel (1868–1870), Amelia Jane (see note 27), Sarah, (see note 144), and Leonard (see note 74). He died at the advanced age of 90½ on July 14, 1929.

86. Private Matthew Bobbett (1899?–1918), Newfoundland Regiment #3541, was the son of John Bobbett of McCallum, Hermitage Bay. He went missing in action in Passchendaele on March 3, 1918, and his body was never found. His name is listed on the Beaumont-Hamel Newfoundland Memorial, France.

87. There were a number of Mrs. Pattens resident in Grand Bank at that time; this reference might be to any number of them. The most likely candidates, however, are either Elizabeth Hickman Patten (1865–1947), wife of John Benjamin Patten (1859–1927), Curt's father's business partner in Patten & Forsey, or Julia Lawrence Patten (1868–1947), mother of his close friend Jack.

I suppose you have some vessels on the western shore this spring have you.

Do you remember the Portuguese that came out in the "Edith Pardy"[88] from Oporto.[89] His name was "Tessier".[90] Well he was killed in the same racket. Poor fellow I think his back was blown off or broken.

Well Dad I guess I'll quit now. Don't worry about me at all. I think I'm safe here.

Give my kind regards to all our people and love to all the family.

I remain your loving Son,
Curt

---

88. One of the deep-sea schooners owned by Patten & Forsey, the *Edith Pardy* was built in Allendale, Nova Scotia, in 1910 and lost at sea near Point aux Gaul, Burin Peninsula, in 1921. It was one of the many Grand Bank vessels that fished the Grand Banks in the spring and summer and carried dried salted cod fish to European markets in the late fall.

89. Oporto (Porto), Portugal, was a regular destination for Grand Bank vessels and their cargoes of dried salted cod fish.

90. Private Joseph Teixeisa (1898?–1918), Newfoundland Regiment #3424, was a native of Oporto, Portugal. He enlisted on January 15, 1917, and his place of residence at the time was Pushthrough, Hermitage Bay. He was killed at Passchendaele on March 13, 1918. His next of kin was his brother, Ignez Teixeisa, of 5759 Rua da Fatica, Oporto. His place of burial is unknown; his name is listed on the Beaumont-Hamel Newfoundland Memorial, France. It is possible, given Curt's spelling of it in his letter as "Tessier," which was most likely based on hearing it, that Joseph's surname was Teixeira, which, unlike Teixeisa, is a common surname in Portugal.

B.E.F.
France
Apr. 3rd/18

Dear Mother,

I received a letter from you yesterday dated Feb 3rd also a parcel containing a pr socks, 2 tins lobster, tin blueberries and a tin of cocoa, and the day before going in the line last time I received two, one containing 2 shirts, helmet and gauntlets, tobacco and chocolates and the other a sleeveless jacket, socks, I tell you the cap and jacket was indeed good as I put it on and while we were in, it was very cold and it helped me a lot. The chocolates were very acceptable, and you can put in as much of it as you can every night time. Don't be particular about shirts, because I only have to carry it when we move anywhere. Send me a nice cake once in a while and tobacco. Don't forget the chocolates when you send one.

We had quite a little rain and cold weather but I managed to stick it OK.

All the boys from GB [Grand Bank] are all safe this time and I think are all right.

How is everybody home. I hear the people are soon going on rations. I wonder if it is true. Food is certainly a problem these days.

We had quite a quite [sic] time in the line this time. Sometimes there wasn't half as much noise as Eleanor could make and other times it wasn't quite as quiet.

How is Grandfather getting along. I suppose he is all right and still keeping to it.

I haven't received Min Hyde's parcel yet but am expecting it every day now and am looking forward to it. I must write Mrs. Patten[91] and thank her for the sweater. It is certainly a good thing, also the helmet.

Christie must certainly be having a good time in Carbonear as she has been there as long. The next thing she will be getting married down there.

I see Pierre Coxworthy quite often. He was here last night when I got my parcel. He had some of the bluberries [sic]. When you send another parcel at any time put in a tin or two of milk and a little sugar if you can spare it. It's very handy indeed.

I suppose Father is very busy now is he with the schooners fitting out. Tell him I shall write him next time.

I guess I'll close now. Remember me to all the people especiall[y] Aunt Mellie and tell her I'll write her soon.

With Love from your Son,
Curt

---

91. Either Elizabeth Hickman Patten or Julia Lawrence Patten. (See note 87.)

B.E.F.
France
May 3/18

Dear Mother,

No doubt you are tired of waiting for a letter from me, but this is really the first chance I have had since writing home last to write.

I am now in hospital for probably a week or so. Not wounded but some kind of a skin disease and the doctor sent me here. It is not serious of course.

Poor Max Clarke got killed in the last racket we were in. He was killed instantly, a sniper got him through the heart as he was helping to get a wounded chap out of a trench. I don't know how I felt when I heard it. I wasn't in the same trench but only about 50 yards away and a wounded chap was crawling out and told me he was killed. I am writing Mr. Clarke and also sending some books I got from his pocket.

Cluett[92] from Garnish was also killed or rather died of wounds. I was quite near him. I heard him cry out and he said he was hit in the stomach. Nobody thought it was serious at all. Two or three days later I heard he had died. He didn't seem very strong at all.

---

92. Private Henry Cluett (1893?–1918), Newfoundland Regiment #3900, son of Annie and Stephen Cluett of Garnish, died of wounds on April 10, 1918, and is buried at La Kreule Military Cemetery, Hazebrouck, France.

I hear they have conscription home now. I suppose Sam will come under that will he. I hope he doesn't as he is rather young yet.

How is everyone home now. I suppose they are all well.

Who do you think I saw day before yesterday - why Allan Parsons.[93] I was very glad to see him indeed he hasn't changed much at all.

I can hardly say how many letters I have received from you since writing last. I have received a good many parcels Millie Dunford's,[94] Hilda Woundy's,[95] two or three from you and Min Hyde's. I shall be writing them the first chance. When I came out of the line the last time I had four waiting for me. That Hold-all was in one of them. I tell you it came in handy as I had just lost all my kit. The cakes were a little smashed up one in was beat to crumbs but never[the]less I could eat it as it was quite a change from Bully and Dog biscuit.[96] The socks were fine. I needed them badly at the time as I had lost everything I own.

May 4

I started this letter yesterday and had to stop so I guess I [will] try & finish it now.

---

93. Allan Parsons (1897–1965), Newfoundland Regiment #4379, was from Harbour Grace.
94. Amelia Forsey Dunford (1900–1972), daughter of Sarah Forsey (1874–1972) and Robert Dunford (1872-1945) of Grand Bank. Her mother, Sarah, was William Forsey's sister. Amelia later married Howard Patten. (See note 143.)
95. Hilda Woundy (1894–1971), a daughter of Elizabeth Lawrence and James Woundy of Grand Bank, and sister of Benjamin Woundy. (See note 159.)
96. Bully beef was a canned corned beef; dog biscuits were hard bread biscuits; both were common fare for soldiers in the trenches in World War I.

It is much colder and raining a little to-day.

It is certainly a nice rest for me here now as we have not been having much rest for the last month and I am enjoying it fine.

How is Sam getting along at school. I hope he doesn't get called up yet a while, although I am very glad I enlisted as a volunteer. It will be a consolation in future days all right to think you had not to be forced.

I hope you have not got uneasy waiting for a letter from me. I have had no chance to write since as we have been on the move ever since I last wrote, however I expect to be able to write more regularly in the future.

Anytime you write me from now on if you got any odd dollar bills or even twenty that you don't want you can just slip them in as an odd dollar comes in handy out here. You get full value for it. Some hopes on the $20 eh.

I got Aunt Martha's[97] address OK, and as we are not far from Paris I shall try and get a few days off to see her. In the meantime I shall write while I am in hospital.

---

97. Martha Louise Buffett Dauphin (1852–1941), was a sister of Curt's grandmother, Christiana Buffett Forsey. Her parents were Sarah Hollett and William Buffett. In the spring of 1873, she met and fell in love with Albert Dauphin, a young businessman from St. Pierre, who was visiting Grand Bank. Her parents became quite upset upon learning that she was pregnant; her father told her to pack all she could of her belongings into a trunk and then took her to St. Pierre, where she and Dauphin were married on July 18. In due course they had five children (Leonce, Gabrielle, Ernest, George and Albert), whom Martha raised "as the only Protestants on St. Pierre." The family eventually moved to Paris, France. Curt's sisters, Christana and Eleanor, visited Leonce in the summer of 1953, while Curt was in England as part of the contingent of Newfoundland veterans who attended the coronation of Queen Elizabeth II. One of Leonce's most treasured possessions was the "God Bless Our Home" cross-stitch that his mother had packed in her trunk when she left Grand Bank.

I have a good chance now to write up my letters as that is about all I have to do besides eat and you might be sure I can do my share of that. The next time you send a box do you think it would be possible to get in some Lemon Pies.[98] Do you think they would keep. One of the cakes I got recently was a little spoiled. Well I think I have written quite a long letter for now as I shall be writing again very soon. Tell Dad not to forget about the odd Dollar bills, American Bills preferred.

With love to all the family

          I remain your Loving Son,

               Curtis

---

98. Lemon Pies: this request is most likely tongue-in-cheek, since a lemon pie would hardly have survived the trip across the Atlantic and subsequent land travel to the Front.

B.E.F.
France
May 17/18

Dear Father,

I wrote you last week from hospital and as I didn't stay as long as I expected I have had to get back with the boys again. I got back day before yesterday OK.

I guess we are out of the line now for quite a while, some say for months as we got quite a cutting up about this time last month that there were hardly any of us left.[99]

So they have taken us out for a rest at General Hdqtrs and we are having a good time indeed.

I will tell you a little about our last engagement with Fritz.

We had just come out of the trenches after 4 days in and thought we were out for a nice little rest and the next thing we knew we had to go right to it that night again. We met him at a railway track that night and believe me he got a warm reception

---

99. On April 9, 1918, after four days on the front line, the Newfoundland Regiment was scheduled for a period of rest. It was much shorter than they had anticipated, as the next day they were ordered to Bailleul, where they encountered German machine-gun fire at the railway station at Steenwerck, a few miles south of Bailleul. A number of the Regiment were killed or injured, but they held on long enough to allow for the safe withdrawal of the British field guns that were in place there. On the 11th, they moved to de Broecken farm to the northeast. Over the next two weeks, the Regiment's C and D companies were involved in heavy fighting, with casualties numbering over 200.

from the Caribou.[100] He left many a man there - they fell just like grass in front of our machine gun fire. Of course we lost a lot too as we had to advance about 600 yards across a field and his machine gun fire was awful, just like rain. They were cutting grass up all around your feet and I tell you what [that] things got nice and lively and sweet.

I didn't really realize where I was. I seemed to have got dazed and mad and just kept going ahead as if nothing was happening. I got hit in the leg once with a piece of shrapnel about 2 inches long. I thought I had a nice Blighty[101] but when I looked the pants weren't even torn. I felt rather disappointed at first as I was getting tired of it, but I guess it's just as well I didn't get one.

Dead men will never bother me after this as now we're out of it I seem to forget all about it. I hope the war will be over before we go in again.

How is Sam getting along. I only hope that he shall never have to come out here as I'm enough for now, but of course if I should get popped off I'd like him to take my place but I hope he doesn't.

Steve Smith got wounded that same day. I don't know whether it was serious or not.

Poor Max Clarke got killed some days later.

A year ago yesterday I left America to come home - Lench reminded me of it to-day. He has been lucky. All the while we were chasing Fritz he was at a signalling school learning signalling, so he got clear of all of it but I [am] glad I had the experience and when

---

100. The caribou is the symbol of the Newfoundland Regiment and is used here as a nickname for the Regiment.
101. See note 78.

Curtis Forsey

I get home I'll be able to go on the stage head with the best of them and spin my yarn.[102]

I hear you are having quite a problem with food home now. Well I only wish I could get home now. Scarce or no scarce, I'd have a feed.

Well I guess I'll close now, with love to all the family and wishing you good luck.

I remain your loving Son,
Curt

---

102. A reference to the men, usually elderly fishermen, who gathered at various stageheads along the Grand Bank waterfront to enjoy each other's company and tell stories of their experiences, some of which often bordered on tall tales.

B.E.F.
France May 21/18

Dear Father,

I received your letter of April 11th to-day. I may say that I was indeed glad to get a letter as it was the first since about Apr. 28 or thereabouts.

I was very glad to hear of all being well as I was beginning to get anxious of not getting any mail for so long a time.

You spoke of getting a field card from me. I had written several letters before that. I was wondering if you had received them or not.

Thornhill has certainly done well again hasn't he. Gosh you people must be tired of making money. Why not have a rest.

I hear to-day where conscription has come into force for good. I'm glad you are too old for it any way. I wonder will Sam be called up. I feel glad to think that at least I volunteered a year, not very long I admit but a good shot from a conscript. But never[the]less they will get as good a show or at least better than the volunteers.

I was rather disappointed at not getting a letter from mother as her letters usually contain the news in detail.

I often wonder if Sam gets my letters. I have written two or three times since coming to this side & have received no reply. I have always written & addressed them to the College[103] but have received no reply.

---

103. Upper Canada Business College, Chatham, Ontario, where Sam was a student.

We are having very warm weather indeed now. In fact I find it almost as warm as in New York.

A year ago tomorrow I left P.A.B.[104] to come here. Some things have happened since then.

It will soon be Empire Day[105] again won't it. I was only thinking of when we were young. How we used to look forward to that day for almost months in advance. I'd have my worms dug at least a week before hand, that was something I always prepared for. I can almost hear mother hollering at me now after having a night out for night worms.

Pierre Coxworthy told me to-day he had seen where Billy Pennell[106] had enlisted. If he has why look out for peace, as no German would ever face him & being of a peaceful occupation (shepherd) he ought to bring his talent into good use. I can imagine him out here now with some of Fritz's 9.2[107] pilching around. I guess it would make Billy feel something like I felt myself at first.

---

104. Port aux Basques.
105. Another name for May 24, Queen Victoria's birthday.
106. Private William J. (Billy) Penwell (1886–1988), Newfoundland Regiment #4583, son of Ann Dodge and John Penwell of Grand Bank. Penwell worked as a sheep herder and attended the Salvation Army College for Officer Training in St. John's before he enlisted in the Newfoundland Regiment. Following the war he was employed in a shoe factory in Detroit and in the coal mines in Glace Bay, Nova Scotia, before returning to Grand Bank where he cared for his elderly mother until her death at age 95, and was the town's only cobbler for many years. Longevity seems to be a trait in his family, as at the time of his death on April 4, 1988, he was just 101 days short of his 102nd birthday, and one of the few members of the Newfoundland Regiment from World War I to pass their 100th birthday.
107. The "9.2" was actually the size of a British Howitzer, a gun with a calibre of 9.2 inches and capable of firing a 290-pound shell. The German equivalent was the 24 centimetre gun made by the armaments manufacturer Krupp of Essen.

Grand Bank Soldier

You know the story Capt Noel[108] used to tell of the recruit for the Boer War[109] - well you have it brought out good. Only of course the same thing hardly happened to me as him.

Well I guess I'll close for now as I wrote only a few days ago and I shall be able to write quite often for a while now. Hope you received all my letters OK, and with love to mother and all the family, I remain as ever

Your loving Son
C. Forsey

P. S. (over)

Will you please send me as soon as you get this some picture post cards of Nfld or if you have a few snaps of you[r] beaches[110] as I met a man in the YMCA tonight and he seems quite interested in home and asked me if I had any. Sorry I didn't have any, but try & send some won't you. Some views of the interior.

Yours
Curt

---

108. Captain Noel – unidentified.
109. The Boer War (1899–1902) was fought between British troops and Boers, white settlers of Dutch extraction who colonized the Orange Free State and the Transvaal, for control of southern Africa and the access to the diamond mines of Rhodesia. The British were eventually victorious, uniting the two former Boer states with its own South African colonies (Cape Colony and Natal) to form the Union of South Africa. A number of Newfoundlanders fought in that war.
110. The stretches of land along the Grand Bank seashore that were covered with beach rocks and used to dry fish. Each of the major fish traders had one or more, and those areas are still identified by some people using those names even though they are now covered with houses and other buildings.

BEF
France
June 7/18

Dear Father,

I received a letter from you to-day written Apr. 27 but imagine now you are in N Scotia as you said you were going in May. I also received three from mother written one Mar 17, another Apr 23, and another sometime in May, a few days previous. No doubt by now you know I have come through all the stunts unhurt. I had some narrow escapes I admit but Fritz couldn't get me.

You spoke in your letter that the news said that Fritz was in Hamel hill. Well Hamel Hill[111] is where I fought, that was where we had our last engagement. I may say we spent 22 days in the hill at one time with a little better than ¼ a loaf of bread a man for a day, with trenches full of mud. You used to tell me I'd sleep in a bucket of water. Well I think if you ever were in my place you would too, for I have often went to sleep a[nd] woken up wet to the skin. I spent four days on Passchendale Ridge[112] wet through in March with no dry clothes to put on, & I tell you it was none too comfortable. It was freezing then.

You seem to say I don't write newsy enough letters. Well I try

---

111. Part of the Battle of Bailleul of March–April 1917. (See note 123.) Hamel Hill is the name of one of the Flanders Hills and should not be confused with Hamel, France.
112. Passchendaele Ridge was a piece of high ground near the Belgian town of Ypres in West Flanders. (See note 133.)

to do my best. You mentioned about John Patten saying I got buried. Well I wrote and told you about that. I don't know whether you received my letters or not but I told you about it. It didn't amount to much. I got buried by a shell that came about 3 feet behind our trench and blew the trench on top of me.[113] I got buried all right but nothing bad. I got clear with a skinned knee so I considered myself lucky. I haven't received any boxes since writing last so I am expecting one every day now. I hope you are not worrying about me now as we are in a safe place for quite a while. We'll meet again soon.

                I remain your loving Son
                        Curt

---

113. No letter appears to have survived in which Curt tells of that experience.

B.E.F.
France
June 15/18

Dear Mother,

I received yours & father's letters yesterday, in fact I received two from you and one from Aunt Mellie. I was glad indeed to hear from her and I shall write her soon.

One of your letters was written May 11/ and the other Apr. 27. Father's was written May 11th, also.

I was glad indeed to hear every body was well home, I often wonder how everybody are. Of course I'm all right here, couldn't be better. Rog Lench & I are going to try and have some photos taken in the near future, so if we succeed I shall send them along. It's pretty hard now to get any taken as everything as you know is upside down.

Yes it was too bad indeed about poor Max Clarke. I know his people must find it hard indeed but still. I suppose it takes men to carry on the racket and you've got to expect such things. Where he is now buried is in German hands.

I was glad indeed to hear the schooners had done well again. I suppose father has been to Shelburne[114] and back by this time. Is it a banker or a foreign schooner they are getting.

---

114. Shelburne is a town on the southeastern coast of Nova Scotia, which boasts that it "has the third best natural harbour in the world." It was a major shipbuilding centre for wooden banking schooners in the 19th and early 20th centuries. At least two Patten & Forsey schooners (*Carrie & Nellie*, *Flowerdew*) and one Wiliam Forsey Ltd. schooner (*Christie & Eleanor*) were built there.

You seem to think I don't write newsy enough letters. Well where we are now there is really not enough happening to talk about. Only Fritz keeps you awake a lot at nights, bombing the town we are in and the ground shakes so you can't go asleep at times. But still I manage to sleep all through the bombardment some nights and the next morning someone will say Fritz was over last night. Did you hear him. I'll say no. He's got to come early when I hear him and besides that we have a battery of anti-air craft guns not far from us and I don't even hear them, so you see I'm as bad as ever. But you get used to all that stuff but wait till I get home and I'll take a week or so off and tell you everything I know about it, & then when I get all the truth told I'll tell lies.

How is Sam getting along. Tell father not to let him enlist if he can help it, but let him join the navy if anything. One of us in this is enough.

Jack, Lench and all the boys from around home are well. Sam Hollett often asks about John Thornhill and the business.[115] I remain

       Your loving Son,
       C. Forsey

---

115. Hollett's curiosity about Captain Thornhill and "the business" would lead one to believe that he may have crewed on one of the Patten & Forsey schooners under Thornhill's command.

B.E.F.
France
July 12/18

Dear Mother,

I received a letter from you a few days ago, also a parcel yesterday. I received two parcels one from Aunt Mellie and one from you. I was very glad indeed to get them as the cake & milk really did come in handy.

This is the first letter I have written for more than a week now. I wrote Christie last. We have moved from where we were so it rather upset correspondence.

This is a grand place where we are now by the sea side.[116] Plenty of bathing and it certainly reminds me of home indeed.

Nearly all the family's birthdays have passed during last month & May. I always thought of them.

Has Sam got into the Army yet. I understood quite awhile ago he was coming home from Toronto to join up. Two Molliers[117] boys

---

116. From May to August 1918, the Newfoundland Regiment was assigned to provide personal bodyguards to Field Marshall Sir Douglas Haig, the Commander-in-Chief of the British Expeditionary Force in France, and also to furnish guards and working parties for the BEF General Headquarters at Montreuil, six miles up the Canche River from the seaport of Étaples. While serving in this capacity, they were billeted at the nearby village of Ecuires, but they underwent training at the tent camp at Camiers, on the French coast, where, in their free time, they could swim in the English Channel.
117. Given the date and the implication from the letter that these men were recent recruits, it is most likely that the four soldiers referred to here

& Joe Lee's[118] son and also a Riggs[119] boy are now in France. I wish I could get a chance to get to Paris & see Aunt Martha but I'm afraid my chances are very slim as no leave will be granted, only at certain times & you have to take your turn for that & of course if I got any leave I would much rather go to England than stay in France, as France is not at all a good country in war time.

How are all the vessels home now. I suppose they have all done good as usual.

I had a letter from Christie some time ago & she told me father was going to build a new one of about 400 tons. She will certainly be a large vessel all right.

No doubt father has been long home from Nova Scotia.

We have had quite a deal of rain lately but it has all cleared of[f] now and fine once more. The weather here is quite good indeed and it is the sort of place you could hold on to for quite a long time.

---

are Berkley Weymouth and Thomas Bennett from Molliers, a small community just north of Grand Bank, and Ben Lee and George Riggs, both from Grand Bank. All four, together with Matthew Hunt from Harbour Breton, enlisted at the same time (they have regimental numbers 4081 to 4085, and would probably have travelled to St. John's together on the same coastal boat in order to join up). Thomas Bennett, who was born in Grand Bank, held Regiment #4084.

Berkley Weymouth (1898-1938), Newfoundland Regiment #4081, was also born in Grand Bank. He eventually returned to Molliers where he and his wife, Laura (1903-1975), became the parents of four children: Bella, Jane Esther, Miriam and Benjamin.

118. Benjamin Lee, Newfoundland Regiment #4082, was the son of Ann Francis and Joseph Lee of Grand Bank. He returned to Newfoundland after the war (see letter dated January 13, 1919, below) but does not reappear in Grand Bank records.

119. George Riggs (1894-1959), Newfoundland Regiment #4085, was the son of Rachel Scott and William Riggs of Grand Bank. After the war he returned to Grand Bank where he and his wife Cecelia raised their family: Fred, Irene, Elizabeth, William, Thomas, Samuel, Annie, Lewis and Margaret.

Curtis Forsey

I suppose there a[re] a lot of boys joining up every day now are there. Well I suppose the sooner they come along the quicker we shall be in the line. There is a strange thing about the line. When you get out of it you seem to want to go back again, and when you're in of course you want to be out.

They say here that we are not expected to be going in the line until the fall. Of course when we do go in of course it's over the top again. I've gone over once & I guess I can do it again.

I am a Lewis Gunner[120] now. I don't know how I'll like it as I was only put on recently. But you can have more fun with one than a rifle in the line.

Will write again soon.

I remain your Son,
Curtis

---

120. Machine gunner.

Lance Corporal Curtis Forsey, Royal Newfoundland Regiment.

FAMILY

Curt Forsey's parents: Sarah Forward Tibbo and William; the woman on the right is Effie Buffett.

Curt as a baby, c. 1896.

The three oldest Forsey children: Sam, Christana and Curt, c. 1902.

William Forsey's Brother, Leonard, his wife Hannah, and their sons Bill (front) and Reuben.

William Forsey's house, Church Street, Grand Bank. On the balcony (l-r): Dr. Claude Buffett, Eleanor Forsey, William Forsey, Sarah Forsey, Helen Buffett, Christana Forsey.

Amelia Foote, Curt's father's sister.

Sarah Forsey, Curt's mother, with her sisters Winifred and Henrietta.

George Dunford.

Samuel Tibbo.

The Grand Bank Methodist schoolhouse Curt attended.

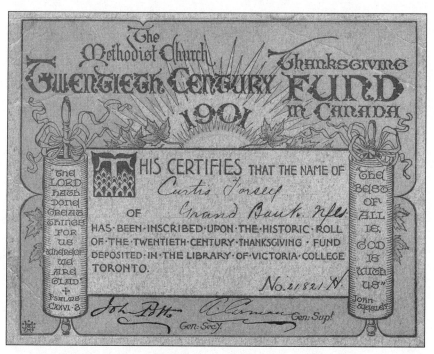

Curt's membership card for the Methodist Church Twentieth Century Thanksgiving Fund.

Curtis Forsey

WORLD WAR I

Corporal Rogerson Lench and Corporal Curtis Forsey.

The Bank of Nova Scotia Connection

Corporal G. Max Clarke.
Killed April 18, 1918.

Private Graham Bennett.

Cadet Benjamin L. Woundy.
Died November 29, 1918.

Private John B. Patten.

These four Grand Bankers were each employed by the Bank of Nova Scotia before joining the war effort. Clarke, Bennett and Patten enlisted in the Newfoundland Regiment; Woundy, the Royal Air Force. The images of Clarke, Bennett and Woundy have been supplied by the ScotiaBank Group Archives, Toronto, Ontario, who have given permission for their reproduction here.

Private Reuben Osborne.
Killed September 29, 1918.

Private Pierre Coxworthy.

CQMS Edward H. Nicholle.
Killed October 10, 1917.

Private William J. Penwell wearing
his Salvation Army cadet uniform.

ROYAL NEWFOUNDLAND REGIMENT

Captain J. J. O'Grady.

2nd Lieutenant Stephen K. Smith.

Sergeant George Tuff.

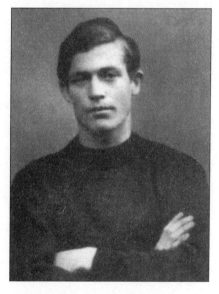

Sergeant William Herbert Lench.

Bletchingley Castle Relief Hospital, where Curt spent several weeks recuperating from his injuries in the fall of 1918.

Curt's discharge certificate from the Royal Newfoundland Regiment.

Curt's membership card for the Great War Veterans' Association of Newfoundland.

The Imperial Tobacco Co. (N.F.) Ltd. Staff Memorial at Beaumont-Hamel Newfoundland Memorial Park, France.

Grand Bank War Memorial.

HOME AGAIN

Curtis Forsey.

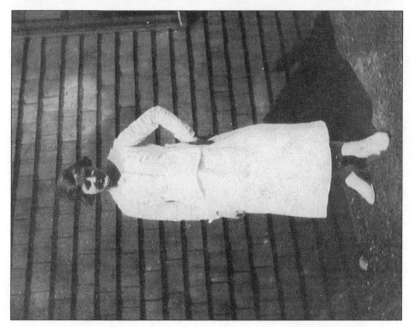

Hazel Tibbo (Curt's wife).

Hazel at Epworth, 1923.

Curt, Helen and Hazel, Epworth, 1923.

Four generations of Forseys (l-r): Pointer John Forsey (Curt's grandfather) holding Helen, William, Curt at Epworth, 1923.

Epworth, 1923 (l-r): Pointer John, Hazel holding Helen, William Forsey, Muriel Tibbo (Hazel's sister), Jack Patten, J. B. Patten (William Forsey's business partner).

Hazel with her four children: Jane, Helen, Amelia and baby Bill, Grand Bank, 1935.

Ches Forsey, Curt's brother.

Christana Forsey (Curt's sister) wedding (l-r): William Forsey, Sarah Forsey, Horatio Oakley (groom), Christana Forsey (bride), Clayton Patten (best man), Eleanor Forsey (maid of honour).

Eleanor L. Forsey, Curt's sister.

Dr. Chester Harris, Royal Army Medical Corps, Eleanor's husband.

Sam Forsey, Curt's brother.

Sam Forsey and Esther Stoodley on their wedding day, October 12, 1932.

Water Street, Grand Bank (l-r): Billy Matthews barbershop, William Forsey, Ltd. and Forward and Tibbo, Ltd.
C. R. TIBBO PHOTOGRAPH.

William Forsey, Ltd. schooner *Helen Forsey*.

Grand Bank Soldier

Grand Bank Town Council, 1948-1952 (l-r): Samuel Stoodley (Councillor), Maxwell Dunford (Deputy Mayor), Curt Forsey (Mayor), Barbara Spencer (Clerk), Percival Hickman (Councillor), Philip Gilliard (Councillor). Missing from picture: Fred Tessier (Councillor).

Grand Bank Branch 24 of the Royal Canadian Legion at the time of the visit of Newfoundland Lieutenant Governor Sir Leonard Outerbride in the early 1950s (front l-r): George Bungay, George Riggs, Curt Forsey (President), Outerbridge, Newton Blagdon, John Ben Anstey, Thomas Burfitt; (back l-r): Rudell Nurse, George Brown, Gordon Weymouth, Samuel Anstey, George Nurse, Max Matthews. All men fought in either World War I or World War II.

Curt, 1960s.

Curt, 1970s on sea wall, Grand Bank.

Curt and Hazel, 1980s.

B.E.F.
France
July 18/18

Dear Father

I received a letter from mother yesterday. She said she was expecting you home the following day after writing, also Sam. Tell Sam to drop me a line when he arrives. I wonder if he will join up. I hope he doesn't have to. I was much surprised at mother not hearing from me for quite awhile.

She spoke of me having some personal property of Max Clarke's. I have but I have understood that I couldn't send it from France so I have been keeping it all the time in hope of giving it to somebody going to England on leave where I think they can mail it.

When I wrote Mr. Clarke[121] I was in hospital and from there I learned it could not be sent. I was sorry to hear of all the deaths home - it must certainly be some epidemic that is going around. The troops were struck somewhat similar to that a month ago. No deaths occurred but it was really bad.

---

121. Lionel P. Clarke (1866-1926) was born in Carbonear. He and his wife, Sarah (1873-1946), who was also from Carbonear, moved to Grand Bank around 1898. Their oldest son, Max, was born in Bonavista in 1897 while their second son, Roy, was born in Grand Bank in 1899. A daughter, Georgina, was born in Bonavista in 1896, while three younger children, Frederick, Lina and Flossie were born in Grand Bank. Clarke went to Grand Bank as a teacher at the Methodist Academy and would have been one of Curt's teachers. The family relocated to Corner Brook some time after 1921, and it was there that both Lionel and Sarah died and were buried.

Was very pleased also to hear the bankers had done so well again but I suppose its needed as such prices there has never been before.

I often wonder whether you receive all my letters or not as often Mother says she hasn't received any for so long a time. Letters are sometimes delayed as yesterday I received one from America written January 22nd so you see such things may happen [to] mine. Sometimes its three weeks & more between your letters.

I don't know when we shall be going in the line again soon & if so I never want to go on the Belgium front again, its certainly a bad place. They say the Somme[122] is quite good. I wouldn't mind that or Italy. They say there is a lot doing there now.

But I suppose it doesn't matter much where you go if you are to get it.

Poor Max Clarke got it didn't he. I shall always feel for that. He was killed just on the aft of Baileiu [Bailleul].[123] The city was in flames at the time. I tell you it was certainly hot around there for awhile.

We are by the sea at present, plenty of bathing and its certainly fine. It rains hard and we are bothered quite a lot with air raids but its much better than shell fire and I prefer it any day.

I wrote mother a few days ago so I suppose you will receive these at the same time. I hope Sam doesn't have to join up for a

---

122. This is certainly an ironic turn of events since the Newfoundland Regiment had suffered so many casulties at Beaumont Hamel, which was part of the original Battle of the Somme, just two years before.

123. Bailleul is a city in northern France, just a few miles from the Belgian border. Its position forms a roughly equilateral triangle with Poperinghe to the north and Ypres to the northeast. It was the site of intense fighting during the spring of 1918, with the Newfoundland Regiment earning the battle honour Bailleul for its heroic stand during the month-long battle. Following this they were given a well-deserved rest at Montreuil. (See note 116.)

while yet as I don't think he could stand France for a couple of years yet. It is certainly hard in the line for one his age although there are younger boys than Sam out here. Still I don't think he is strong enough.

I am a Lewis Gunner now. Don't know whether I will take it in the line or not. It is a thing you can do a lot of damage with all right and I feel I owe them a lot and if I go in again, and can get a chance I [will] pay up for a lot.

I remain Your Son,
Curtis

B.E.F.
France
26/7/18

Dear Father,

Have received no letter from you for a long while but suppose you are too busy at present to attend to it. I received a letter from Christie a few days ago. I notice Sam has gone to Burin. Hope he will do good there. Is he there all alone or has he some help.

Was very glad to hear that the vessels had done extremely well. I guess at the end of the year they will be even better than last year.

I have not received any parcels for quite a long while. No doubt I shall soon get one again soon. I am not with the battalion at present so that makes my mail a little longer in reaching me but no doubt in the near future I shall be getting one.

By Christie's letter it seems that you have just got back from St. John's. You seem to be doing a lot of travelling, this year more so than any other. But I suppose the increase in business demands it.

Things are very quiet around here at present. Not much news and nothing very exciting happening only an occasional air-raid.

The weather continues to keep warm, in fact sometimes it is too warm.

I will be writing again soon. I am also writing Sam this week. With best wishes and love to all the family.

I remain Your Son,
Curtis

3828 C. Forsey
"D" Company
First Royal NFLD Regiment
B.E.F.
July 28/18 France

Dear Father,

I received a letter from Mother & Sam on the 25th, a parcel yesterday and your registered letter last night, so you see in the last few weeks I have done extremely good.

Things are much the same around here now, not many changes. I was down to a village about 3 miles from here last week to see Aaron Tibbo,[124] so if you see Mr. Tibbo[125] tell him I saw Aaron. No doubt though he has written home & mentioned it.

The war news these days seems rather encouraging. I expect if we get Fritz on the run it won't be so hard then, but the trouble is getting him going.

Well I'm a Lewis Gunner now and take it from me, if I get fair

---

124. Aaron Grandy Tibbo (1892-1948), son of Hannah Grandy and Samuel Tibbo of Grand Bank. He was in Halifax working as a baker when the war broke out and enlisted there in the Canadian Expeditionary Force, #469152, on August 13, 1915. He returned to Grand Bank after the war and married Linda Jane Pardy (1901-1982).

125. Samuel Tibbo (1853-1934) was the father of George P. Tibbo and Aaron G. Tibbo. He married Hannah Grandy (1856-1934) of Garnish on December 16, 1884. Their other children were Frederick (1888-1986), Esther Azalea (1891-1935), Benjamin Buffett (1896-1919), Donald W. (1899-1986), and Elsie (1903-1996).

play in the line and a shell don't get me, I'll have some fun with it. It's a very destructive weapon. I've seen them fall like sheep in front of it, so I'm going to try and see what I can do when we get in again.

I was very pleased to hear that the vessels have done so well again this spring no doubt they will keep it up.

I note that Sam was going to Burin. I suppose he will go there to work in this new place you have taken over is he.

He said in his letter he had registered and that he was going to wait until he is called up. Well I hope he doesn't have to come, as I'm afraid he [will] find it hard and I doubt whether he could stand it. Couldn't you claim to keep him home on account of me being out here now. Will they take two brothers where there are only two.

Mother was asking for my picture. Well I'm going to try and get some but as you know it's very hard now, as everything out here is on the bum, but some places you can get some taken on cards but they are not good by any means. But I suppose they would be much better than nothing.

I thought I would get a chance to see Aunt Martha but I'm afraid I won't unless I get in hospital somewhere in the vicinity of their town. Then if I get hit out here I'd rather go to England, as it's bad enough here the best of times but now it's completely gone on the bum.

I must now thank you for the $20 you sent me. I assure you it came in handy and I am very thankful.

I suppose Sam is having a whale of a time home now is he. No doubt he rather be in the Regiment but never mind. Anywhere in Nfld is far better than Passchendaele Ridge and Armentieres,[126] so let him stay home as long as he can.

---

126. Armentières is best remembered today for the popular World War I marching song "Mademoiselle from Armentières." This town in the north of

Thanking you again for your present & with love to all the family.

I remain your Son,
Curtis

France on the Belgian border was the site of tremendous fighting during the war. So great were the losses sustained by the townspeople that Armentières was presented with both the British Military Cross and the French Legion of Honour, and it is the location of several military cemeteries containing the last remains of troops of many nations who were killed in the area.

B.E.F.
France
Aug 14/18

Dear Mother,

I received your letter a few days ago, was glad indeed to hear once again. It was so long since I heard.

I have received no parcels lately. The sooner one comes along the better as I'm badly in need of socks at present.

The weather is quite warm again now. In fact it is almost unbearable at times.

I was very glad to hear that the vessels had done well again. Good luck seems to follow them right through.

I noticed by your letter yesterday that father was in St. John's but no doubt he is back again. The $20 was very acceptable indeed so you can imagine how I enjoyed having it.

I suppose Sam is still in Burin is he. I suppose he is going to stay there all the time is he until he gets called up, which I hope will be a very long time yet.

Christie I guess will be in Sackville[127] before this letter arrives. I will write her soon.

How is Ches & Eleanor. They too I suppose have grown a lot since I left home too.

A lot of the first boys have gone home from here. No doubt they

---

127. Sackville, New Brunswick, where Christana had gone to attend Mount Allison University.

have arrived home by this time. I don't know how long they will be gone I'm sure.

It must certainly be good for them to get home after being away for so long. By the time I'm gone as long as they have I shall be glad too I suppose.

News is very scarce indeed these days, nothing in particular happening. Will write again soon.

Your Son,
Curtis

3828 L/C C. Forsey B.E.F
"D" Coy France
Royal NFLD Regmt Sept 5/18

Dear Mother,

I have received no letters since writing last. I am away at present from the battalion and no doubt my mail is more delayed than it would be otherwise.

Yesterday I received a parcel containing a pr. of socks and some home-made preserves, also coffee & milk and a few toilet articles. I think some of them were from Aunt Min.[128]

About a week ago I got one containing a cake alone. The cake was very good indeed but I think it would have been better only it was quite a long time on the way.

No doubt Christie is in Sackville. I think I shall drop her a line to night. I wrote Sam last week and I suppose he will answer it if he receives it. I addressed it to Epworth,[129] no doubt that will get him OK.

So there are only four of you altogether home now Eh. Quite

---

128. Mary Tibbo Forward (1873–1962) was a sister of Curt's mother, Sarah Tibbo Forsey. She married Charles Forward (1875–1972) in 1907, the year before he and her brother, Felix Tibbo, established Forward & Tibbo, which was involved in the deep-sea fishery and operated a general merchandise business. (See note 152.)

129. Epworth is a small community on the eastern side of the Burin Peninsula, near Burin. Patten & Forsey had a branch of its business in the community.

a difference indeed to what it used to be say eight or ten years ago.

Father no doubt is quite busy these days as usual.

I imagine Sam must be a busy man these days too. Write and tell me the nature etc. of the business he has to do next time and tell him I want a box of tobacco from him. I forgot to mention it to him last time. Tell him to mark it socks or cake as if tobacco was named on the package I'd never get it.

How is Grandfather getting on same old gr[andfather] I guess and working just as hard as usual.

I was mighty glad indeed to get that $20 bill some time ago. There was hardly any need of sending so much. Anytime any small change is in your way send them P. F. [Patten & Forsey] or Buffett's Register tickets will do.

It is now about 1:30 am and I'm on duty to night. The nights seem rather long especially when you have nothing to do.

I don't know when we shall become a fighting unit again I'm sure. But I expect sometime in the near future.

The War News seems very good indeed these days, for how long it's quite hard to say.

So Urs Janes[130] is engaged Eh. Well I can hear the old woman and Uncle Bill[131] arguing now. I bet it is quite a circus at times.

---

130. Ursula Janes Squires (1897–1992), daughter of Avelina Bond (1874–1946) and George Janes (1867–1898) and granddaughter of Jane Stoodley and William Bond. Before her marriage to Cyril Squires (1896–1963), a deep-sea fishing captain originally from Pool's Cove, Fortune Bay, she worked as a nursemaid for the Forsey family. She had one sibling, a brother, Bob. (See note 16.)

131. Jane Stoodley Bond (1841–1919?) was a daughter of Eleanor Rose (1816–1893) and George Stoodley (1809–1893), and the wife of William Bond (1835–192?). According to Christana Forsey Oakley, "Their house was

Curtis Forsey

I guess I'll close for now with love to all the family.

> I remain Your Son,
> Curtis

---

like a drop-in centre and the boys would try to get Jane and Bill arguing." An interesting and cheap form of entertainment in the days before radio and television! (See note 69.)

\# 3828
L/C C. Forsey B.E.F
"D" Company France
1st Royal N.F.L.D. Regmt Sept 16/18

Dear Mother,

    I have received no letter since writing last. I am still away from my batt[alion] on duty but am leaving to-morrow to join them in the line.

    If you don't hear from me for a couple of weeks this time don't worry as I may not get the time to write regular for a little while.

    The weather keeps up quite warm here yet but the nights are very cold indeed. I believe we are going to have quite a hard winter this year. I only hope I can escape it, and spend it in England or somewhere clear of France.

    I have received no letter from Father for quite a long while. I suppose he is still busy and cannot find time to write.

    I wrote Christie last week and addressed it to Sackville. I imagine she will get it OK.

    I also wrote Sam a few weeks ago and he no doubt will get it as well. I guess he is having a good time at Burin. He's certainly lucky and he ought to appreciate it.

    I have received no parcel since writing last either but expect to get both mail & parcel when I get back with the boys.

    Jack Patten, Lench and all the boys from home were quite well the last time I saw them, and I guess they are still going good.

Curtis Forsey

How are all the family. I suppose they are still going good are they.

Trusting this gets you OK, and I shall try and get time to write in the near future.

I remain Your Son,
Curtis

35 General Hospital[132]
France
Oct. 5/18

Dear Father,

No doubt for quite a while you have been waiting for a letter from me, especially knowing I have been wounded, but you can stop worrying now as you can rest assured I am OK.

I suppose you would like to know a little about the stint would you.

Well to begin with we went in the trenches on the night of Mother's birthday Sept 20th. We went there expecting to attack next on Sunday morning but somehow didn't and we stayed then until Saturday morning and then it started. Our trenches were dug directly in front of Ypres.[133] I may say that the trench I was in was through a graveyard (civilian).

Our barrage opened out at daybreak and over we went with the Belgians on our left, and believe me twas a barrage.

We continued to advance until about noon with no resistance until we gained our final objective.

---

132. British Expeditionary Force casualty hospital at Boulogne, France.
133. Ypres (commonly called Wipers in the period following the war) is a town in West Flanders, Belgium, which was the site of three major battles during the war. It was the third battle at Ypres (July 21–November 6, 1917), the October and November part of which is also known as the Battle of Passchendaele, that resulted in the Allied forces securing the area, which eventually enabled them to make advances in Flanders and northern France.

Another body of troops passed through us and kept up the advance.

Sunday morning came and we went over again without any barrage as our artillery had not shifted up.

The Germans started to shell us and give us some hot machine gun fire. A lot of our men died that day. Anyway first of all I got a piece of shrapnel in the ankle but continued to carry on until 11 o'clock when I got two bullets in the left thigh about a foot below the hip bone. I fell into a shell hole full of water when I got it and of course that soaked me.

Then I turned to get back before the wounds got stiff.

Well I walked for about 2 hours and came to a Belgian dressing station but it was filled up & I got taken aboard of a car & taken down to Ypres and got my dressing done.

I had a box from home before going in with a towel in it so tell Mother when I got hit first that was what I used as a dressing. I was in front of Roulers[134] when I got it. No doubt you are very interested in this advance as I believe it will mean a lot.

I don't know I [am] sure if I will get to Blighty. I hope I do as I'm about sick of France. I have no pain at all so you can rest easy.

I'm expecting to go under operation this afternoon. I was warned for it a long time ago but they haven't come for me yet.

On Friday, September 13, 1918, the Newfoundland Regiment, as part of the 9th Division under the command of General Sir Hugh Tudor (1871-1965), were dispatched to a section of the front to the east of Ypres. It was there, during September and October, that the Regiment took part in fighting at Polygon Wood, Keiberg Ridge, Ledeghem, St. Catherine Cappelle, Ingoyghem, pushing the Germans out of Belgium, closer and closer to their own border. It was at Keiberg Ridge on September 29 that Curt sustained the injuries that would place him in hospital for the remainder of the war.
134. Roulers is the French spelling for Roeselare, a town in the Belgian province of West Flanders.

I wonder how Jack and Rog Lench and Ren Riggs got along. I haven't heard a word about them. I hope they are alright.

Rheub Osmond[135] was killed and also Douglas[136] from Brunette. Osmond I think was killed the first day.

It is so long since hearing from home that I don't know how she is going at all.

This is very poor writing I know but it's the best I can make of it in bed. Will write again soon.

I remain Your Son,
Curtis

---

135. Private Reuben Osborne (1898-1918), Newfoundland Regiment #3421, son of Frances and John Osborne of Grand Bank, was killed at Keiberg Ridge, near Passchendaele, Belgium, on September 29, 1918. Part of the shell that killed Osborne hit Curt in the ankle. Reuben Osborne is buried at Birr Cross Roads Cemetery, Belgium. His father was originally from Stone's Cove, in the bottom of Fortune Bay, near the western entrance to Long Harbour, and his mother was from Mose Ambrose, near the southwest side of the entrance to Fortune Bay. The family arrived in Grand Bank in 1911 from Hoop Cove, which was also situated on the west side of Long Harbour. Although often referred to as Osmond in Grand Bank, the family name was Osborne. His brother, Wilson Osborne (1900-1980), was Grand Bank's last blacksmith, operating from his forge on Water Street until the late 1960s.

136. Private Aaron Keeping Douglas (1896?-1918), Newfoundland Regiment #2904, son of Sarah Jane Keeping and Andrew Douglas of Brunette Island, was killed when a discarded shell exploded at Keiberg Ridge, near Passchendaele, Belgium, on September 29, 1918. He is buried at Dochy Farm New British Cemetery, Belgium. His name is incorrectly listed as Andrew Douglas on the plaque attached to the Grand Bank War Memorial.

Bethnal Green Military Hospital[137]
Cambridge Road
London
E2

Oct 14/18

Dear Father,

I wrote you from France about a week ago, informing you I was all right, and expressing a hope that I would get to "Blighty" which you can see I did.

No doubt you have been informed that I have been [injured] by cable as the first thing they wanted to know when I arrived here who was my next of kin, so doubtless you have been informed.

Well now that I am over here the censorship is not in the way of telling any news, so I will give you a little description of the modern battle.

As you know we had been out for a rest this summer in the city of Montreuil,[138] about 10 miles from Etaples,[139] and some 20 miles

---

137. Bethnal Green is a part of the City of London. An infirmary had been established there between Cambridge Heath Road and Russia Lane in 1882, with a capacity for 750 patients. During World War I it became Bethnal Green Military Hospital.
138. Montreuil (Montreuil-sur-Mer), a city in Pas-de-Calais, in northwest France, situated on the banks of the Canche River, some six miles from the seaport of Étaples. It was the headquarters of the British Army during World War I.
139. Étaples (Étaples-sur-Mer), a seaport near the mouth of the Canche

from Boulogne.[140] We certainly had a rest, but we played peace time soldier there doing guards etc. for the General Staff & Sir Douglas Haig.[141]

At last the time came when we had to take up fighting again. Of course Ypres was where we had to go so on Friday night Sept. 20, Mother's birthday, we went up through the ruins & took up a position in a civilian graveyard. That of course was our reserve line, some of our boys were in the front line.

The Belgians were on our left and the remainder of the 2nd Army was on our right. We were rather a connecting line between the Belgians & British.

We knew we had to go over some time, but nobody knew exactly, so at last Friday night the 27 we were told that we had to go over in the morning.

The Belgians about 2 in the morning put up a terrific bombardment and it stopped about 4:30.

Well at 5:30 we had to go, and it was certainly an awful feeling

---

River, in the Pas-de-Calais in northwest France. It was a stop on the railway line between Boulogne and Amiens and during the war was the principal depot used by the British Army in transporting troops to and from the front lines in northern France. As a result of this, it was a target for repeated enemy bombings, and was awarded the French Croix-de-Guerre in 1920 for the hardships it and its citizens had endured.

140. Boulogne (Boulogne-sur-Mer), located to the northwest of Montreuil, on the English Channel, was the major French seaport destination for troops leaving England intended for action on the Western Front, and the starting point for those returning to England for either hospitalization or leave.

141. Field Marshall Sir Douglas Haig (1861–1928), a career soldier, was appointed Commander-in-Chief of the British Expeditionary Force, including the Newfoundland Regiment, in December 1915, a position he retained until the end of the war. In 1924 he visited Newfoundland, where he unveiled the National War Memorial in St. John's. The following year he officiated at the opening of the Newfoundland Memorial at Beaumont-Hamel Park in France.

to know you had to expose yourself to such fire, so the time gradually came. "5 minutes to go" was the order passed down, then two, and then our barrage opened the biggest one that was ever put up they say.

Any way over we went with our shells going over our head and playing in Fritz's front line & supports.

As we advanced the barrage kept moving forward. When we got over there was nothing left of it. They had all fled.

They showed no fight at all on Saturday and our casualties were very slight.

You couldn't hear any one speak at all, and here you were half choked with smoke & powder, and then it started to rain. Everybody was soaking to the skin & I tell you it was none to comfortable. However we carried on until 2 in the afternoon, dug in and had a little sleep as we certainly needed it.

Well next day being Sunday we had to have another go at it without a barrage.

We went over again and I tell you he started to shell us and give us lots of rifle & machine gun fire & made things rather hot.

We started to loose [sic] quite a few men as we went.

So about 11 or 12 I felt something strike my thigh, it didn't hurt much but I fell into a shell hole and that being full of water I got another soaking.

I took down my pants and here it was three bullet holes — two had struck me and went in the same hole and came out separate.

I was bleeding a good deal & decided to come out. First thing I looked for was a cigarette and then I found they were wet also my tobacco so I managed to bum one and tried to get out.

I crawled walked ran and did everything I could to get clear of it before the wounds got stiff.

I took the Menin road[142] & got out somehow, & you talk about dead Germans. They were all over that road on top of each other and every how. I believe you could have loaded a large schooner.

I went about 5 miles like that until I got to a Belgian Dressing Station & that was full of wounded Belgians so they told me to walk on for another mile & I would find another station.

I just started out when a chaplain saw me and asked what was wrong etc. and with that he put me in his auto and carried me right down to Ypres. It was certainly a good lift.

I got dressed there and put aboard a Red Cross train & sent down the line to Boulogne.

I thought at first that I wouldn't get to Blighty but the nurses said I'd have to have an operation first as my wounds were very dirty. So I had one & got shipped across.

Well you can imagine how I feel being away from it, & I hope that before I am able to go out again it is over.

It's rather tiresome laying in bed all day. I hope I shall soon get up.

The wound in my ankle is not much and is nearly well.

Do you think that it will soon be over. I hope it does & I suppose so do you.

I shall never be sorry of my experiences. Hungry, cold, tired & sleepy as I have been but you can only live in hope. That is the only thing that keeps one alive out there.

You get used to seeing dead men and all the horrible sights, but an empty stomach you never can.

---

142. The Menin Road was located near Ypres, Belgium, where three separate major battles took place during World War I. The road was regarded as one of the most dangerous parts of the Western Front because of the constant German artillery bombardment that was aimed at it.

Curtis Forsey

I wondered that Sunday after I got hit and I had nothing to eat since 4 o'clock Saturday evening what you were going to have for dinner, & if I could only drop in.

Well I hope to some day anyway, the sooner the better.

I remain Your Son,
Curtis.

Bethnal Green Military
Hospital
Cambridge Road
London
Oct. 22nd/18

Dear Mother,

I recieved Aunt Min's parcel about a week ago. I received a letter of yours written in August, a few day[s] late[r] one written September 6 - and yesterday one written Sept. 19, so you see I am beginning to get some of my mail in.

I note on your letter yesterday that father was away. He has done a lot of that this year hasn't he.

Sam I see is at Burin, also note Howard Patten[143] is there with him. I see they must have some nice times together I don't think.

I am still in bed with my wounds but expect to get up soon and get about with a stick, and then I shall go to Convalescent and then I get 10 days leave before going back to Winchester.

I am cabling this weekend for a little money. It would be very

---

143. Howard Patten (1902–1979), son of Elizabeth Hickman and John Benjamin Patten of Grand Bank. The elder Patten and Curt's father, William Forsey, were the founders of the Grand Bank general mercantile firm of Patten & Forsey in 1895. The partnership was dissolved in 1922, with each of the founders establishing their own businesses. Howard, a pharmacist who operated a drugstore in Grand Bank (the first on the Burin Peninsula), acquired control of his father's business, J. B. Patten Sons, some time after the latter's death in 1927. At the time this letter was written, 16-year-old Howard was working at the Patten & Forsey branch in Epworth. (See note 94.)

rotten going around with no money so I'll be very pleased & thankful if I get it.

Well I am feeling quite fit again now. I'm getting rather tired of laying in bed but its a good rest & I'd much rather be in London than France, as it is so desolate now.

I believe the war will soon be over, as it seems that Germany is about settled now since she has abandoned the Belgium coast.

I also heard from Christie a[t] Sackville the second day she arrived so I wrote her. I hope she likes it all right. But I hope she will not be as lonesome as I was when I went there.

How are the people home now.

Grandfather I hope is well and keeping up as usual. You spoke on your letters of not writing and so one can't seem to realize how hard it is to find time & write everybody when you're over there.

But of course I sent Aunt Min and Aunt Sarah Dunford[144] a field card when I was in Poperinghe[145] (Belgium) last winter with a lot more cards I got hold of.

I'm inclined to think a lot of my mail has never reached home. Will write again soon.

                   with love from Your Son,
                   C. Forsey

---

144. Sarah Maria Forsey Dunford (1874–1972) was Curt's father's sister. She married Robert Dunford (1872–1945); they were the parents of one daughter, Amelia (see note 94), and two sons, Maxwell and Leonard.

145. Poperinghe is situated in the Belgian province of West Flanders, some ten kilometres west of Ypres. Except for a brief period at the beginning of the war when it was occupied by German forces, after October 15, 1914, it remained under the control of the Allied forces, which had a base of operations there for most of the war. It was a favourite destination for soldiers who were on short periods of rest leave from the trenches, especially Talbot House, or Toc H, as it was popularly known.

Bethnal Green Military Hosp.
Cambridge Road
London E2
Oct. 30/18

Dear Father,

I have received no letters since hearing last so I am expecting letters now every day. The last letter I had was written Sept. 6 I think so I guess there ought to be more somewhere else by this time.

I noticed that you were not home when I received the last letter but suppose you are now though.

I am getting along fine now. My wounds are healing very quick indeed, much quicker than I expected so I guess in about another week I will be going to Convalescent and have about 3 or 4 weeks there and then I will go back to the depot and then I suppose out to France again.

I kind of hate the idea of going back again after you once get wounded. You find it very hard the second time again as you know what it is like.

I shall never forget that day a month ago yesterday that I got it. The dead were as thick and men dying all around. It was certainly an awful sight. Sometimes in the night I think of it, and it gives me the creeps but still you get used to that as well as anything.

The news certainly seems good these days. I sometimes think that it will soon be over. Well the sooner the better.

I am now able to walk out with a little energy. Of course I limp but I generally go out for 2 hrs in the afternoon.

About a hundred of us here went out one night last week to an "At Home" given by some people in this vicinity. We had a good time indeed. So I think to night they are coming to the hospital and give a kind of entertainment. I hope they do as it breaks the monotony of this place.

I heard from Rog Lench a few days ago. He is all right so far, but Jack Patten is wounded slightly on the ear but I don't think it is enough to get to England with.

Mother has been asking for my picture. I didn't get it taken in France but I will now that I am in England.

I wired for £6 a few days ago, as I get 14 days leave when coming out of hospital and I haven't much money coming to me at the pay office. I really need a little money.

I am very glad that you have managed to keep Sam out of this affair. I shouldn't like to see him in it as I am enough.

I heard from Christie, a letter over a week ago from Sackville.

Will write again soon.

I remain Your Son,
Curtis

              Bletchingley Castle
              Relief Hospital[146]
              Bletchingley
              Surrey
              England
              Nov. 12/18

Dear Father,

I received your cable last night about 8 o'clock. Evidently the first news you heard of my being wounded was my letters.

Well you can see by my address that I have changed over.

I arrived here this morning from London. It's only about 1 hrs ride from London Bridge so this is where I am spending my convalescence. It's a nice country town and the house (hospital) is rather down in a valley, and the scenery is just fine. Food is good indeed and I think I will be able to pick up nicely in a few weeks. My wounds are not all healed yet, in fact my ankle wound is far from well and wearing a boot hurts it. My thigh is not very good either and have a little trouble at times but I guess two or three weeks will find me up OK.

Great excitement prevailed yesterday when the news arrived that armistice had been signed. London simply went mad and have not quite forgotten it yet.

---

146. Bletchingley Castle Relief Hospital was not a real castle but a manor house located in Bletchingley, Surrey, just southwest of London. The hospital, operated by a Mrs. Brandt, had accommodation for 20 convalescing patients.

Germany must indeed be in an awful plight, and now that the Kaiser had abdicated[147] and fled to Holland, it will no doubt be better for the country.

Upon receipt of your cable and seeing that a reply was prepaid I cable[d] you this morning before leaving London for eight pounds.

It seems rather strange to me that you had not received my cable about a week ago, as I cabled you from the Pay Office[148] about the 1st Nov. so evidently you did not get it. So I cabled you again last night.

I received a letter from you a week ago dated Aug 26 that of course was very old and on the same day I heard from Mother written Oct. 6. I was surprised then that you had not received the casualty list. I am very anxious indeed to hear from Rog Lench. I heard from him Oct. 19 and he was alright then but since then Oct. 25 - they had a nasty time[149] and I'm wondering all the time if he's all right.

---

147. Kaiser Wilhelm II (1859–1941), who succeeded his father, Frederick III, as Emperor of Germany in 1888, is often characterized as a leader who precipitated war in Europe in 1914. It would appear that he had much less influence than once thought, with real power in Germany being concentrated with the generals in charge of the German army. As it became more and more evident in the autumn of 1918 that the war was drawing to a close, he was forced to abdicate. The announcement of his abdication was made on November 9, 1918, although Wilhelm did not sign the formal proclamation of that abdication until November 30. He spent the remainder of his life in exile in Holland.
148. The Pay and Records Office for the Newfoundland Regiment was originally located at 34 Victoria Street, while the Newfoundland War Contingencies Office was at 58 Victoria Street, Westminster, London. They both eventually operated out of 58 Victoria. Shortly after the end of the war, that address became the office of Newfoundland's first High Commissioner to Great Britain, Sir Edgar R. Bowring (1858–1943).
149. A reference to the fighting the Regiment was involved in as they advanced from along the Harlebeke road from Vichte to Ingoyghem on October 25 and 26, 1918. On the 27th the Regiment was relieved and given

John Patten I heard was wounded slightly but not enough to get to England.

Well I suppose it should soon be all over with. I am glad I don't have to go back again. If I do I guess it shall be only for working parties or something of that sort. Any how I doubt if there will ever be any more fighting.

I received a box from mother three days ago with a pair of socks etc. I guess it was my birthday box as it contained cards.

Sam I am glad to hear is exempted and will surely not come now as England stopped all recruiting last night.

It is pretty hard on a chap now to get killed or wounded seriously isn't it. I'm certainly thankful I got of[f] as easy as I did.

I remain Your Son,
Curtis

---

a well-deserved rest behind the lines. The fighting of the 25th and 26th would prove to be the Regiment's last, as the Armistice of November 11 was signed while it was still behind the lines.

Bletchingley Castle Relief Hospital
Bletchingley
Surrey
Nov. 17/18

Dear Mother,

I wrote father last Tuesday in reply to his cablegram, and yesterday I received two letters from him, one written October 6 and the other October 12 - on which he said that he had been notified that I had been wounded. I would like for you to keep that telegram and also my name as it appeared in the casualty list for a souvenir.

Well I suppose the thing is over now as it appears that Germany is about finished. I tell you I'm not sorry. I would never want to go through such experiences again for any money, but never[the]less I am not sorry for my experiences, and I wouldn't take any money for them.

But the poor fellows that are to stay out there, is what makes the thing sad. When I think of all I saw die and blown almost to pieces, I think it is marvellous that so many escape.

The Convalescent home I am in is in the valley and it is simply great. Very quiet and the air seems so pure. I believe that if Ches could only come to such places, I'm almost sure he would pick up and perhaps be cured of asthma.

I'm so glad that Sam got clear of it. I used to think sometimes if he came out, I'd have no peace as I'd always been looking after his comfort, and worrying about him, but however he got clear of it: & I'm not sorry.

It certainly must be hard to get knocked out on the end of it all right. I saw yesterday where an officer in the Irish Guards who had been wounded 9 times got killed the last day. That I think is almost too much.

My wounds are getting along nicely. They still have to be dressed daily but improving nicely especially since I came here not a week ago.

This hospital I was in in London wasn't so bad. It was a military and not a V.A.D.[150] and they were very strict.

But now I can walk as much as I like, and have no pain at all & I think in a couple of weeks I shall be able to go on leave.

It is so nice here that I dread to leave it. There is one consolation that I won't fight anymore and I haven't got to go to France although I might have to but not on the same business.

I sometimes think that if I got a good position over here I'd stay for a few years, especially in France as there will be such a demand for men of all kinds & trades. But of course they will send all colonials home for discharge as they are only signed on for duration.

I am anxiously awaiting a reply from Lench. I wrote him a little while ago. I hear the boys have had a hard time & I fear something has happened to him. I wouldn't have anything happen [to] him for anything.

You spoke in your letter about me not saying anything about

---

150. The Voluntary Aid Detachment (VAD) was formed by the British Red Cross and the Order of St. John of Jerusalem in 1909. Thousands of women from all parts of the Empire, including Newfoundland, served in World War I as VAD nurses, ambulance drivers, kitchen and household staff, clerks and fundraisers. For more information see *Your Daughter Fanny: The War Letters of Frances Cluett, VAD*, Bill Rompkey and Bert Riggs (eds.), Flanker Press, 2006, for a first-hand account of a Newfoundland VAD.

Aunt Susie's[151] death. I think I have spoken of it to you at several times. I remember you telling me on your letter when she died & I'm sure I spoke of it on your next letter.

You asked me on one of your letters that I received up in Belgium at one time for a lock of my hair. Well it happened that I had my hair cut just before it and since then well I didn't forget it but I simply didn't want to. It seemed to me as if you thought I wasn't to come out of it, & I felt so miserable at the time. Several times I intended doing it but I couldn't bear the thought of doing it.

However the thing is now over and I guess there isn't so much danger.

Funny thing all the while I was out there in the trenches, especially under heavy shell fire I had a dread all the time of being killed but something told me that it was all right, that I was going to pull through.

Did I tell you that the shell that killed Rheub Osmond wounded me in the ankle. I was about 50 feet from him and saw him fall. Guess I'll close now as I want to write Christie.

I remain Your Son,
Curtis

---

151. Susan Collins (1846–1917), a widow, although not an immediate family relation, lived with Curt's parents at various times during his childhood. She was widowed young and spent the remainder of her life living in and assisting a circle of her friends and relatives with general housework and childcare during pre- and postnatal periods. She is buried in the same plot as Curt's parents.

Bletchingley Castle Relief Hospital
Bletchingley
Surrey
Nov. 26/18

Dear Father,

I received two letters from you a short time ago - one was written Oct. 5/18 and the other on the 12/. Yesterday I received a letter from Mother written on the 15th. Needless to say I was glad indeed to hear that all the family was well and that you were not at all worried about me as the casualty list reported my wounds mild.

I am afraid that it really wasn't as mild as one might expect as the wounds were dirty and I had to have an operation and have them cleaned. They are not healed up yet but now it is only a matter of a few days & I shall be OK and able to go on leave.

As you can see I am still at Convalescent but expect next week I shall go away & return to my unit.

Was glad to hear Sam was doing well & hope he continues so.

Father you seemed rather disappointed that I should get wounded as you said "at the best part of the war". You can hardly imagine my feelings when I got hit. To think I was getting away from it (I don't mean I was afraid) for a rest. We were all dead with hunger and cold, sleeping on the ground every night for 10 days with scarcely anything to eat, & then to know suddenly that that night you would sleep with two or three blankets around you. I tell you its a fine feeling.

I saw by the papers yesterday that Nflders were into Brussels when King Albert entered. I suppose that is a great honour.

To tell the truth I would like to be there but still I've seen enough of it, and Belgium has no attractions for me as I spent almost too much time there.

I wrote Christie a few days ago. I guess I shall soon hear from her again.

The family I suppose is quite small now is it with only two of us left and you and mother. Don't you really enjoy it more now with no charm around.

One thing rather amused me on the morning I got wounded. The Belgians were putting up an awful bombardment and you simply couldn't hear yourself or any one else speak. We were just getting ready to jump the parapet when a fellow says to me "a Hell of a wedding on the left this morning".

There are a couple of more boys here from Nfld but I don't know them. They came from North. I think they are only slightly wounded. I have heard no news from Rog Lench yet. Jack Patten I know was wounded slightly in the ear, but I haven't heard a word from Rog Lench. I wrote him about two weeks ago & have received no reply. However, I hope he is alright. I should feel bad if anything happened to him.

Douglas from Brunette was killed the same day I was wounded, also Rheub Osmond.

Does Ches still have asthma? I believe that if he could only come to such a place as this he would certainly improve. I myself have picked up wonderfully since coming here, as when I came from France I was all in. We get pretty good food indeed and have all kinds of games etc. which make the time pass very quickly.

How is Uncle Fel and Aunt Ellie.[152] Remember me to them.

---

152. Felix G. Tibbo (1879-1958) was Curt's uncle, his mother, Sarah Tibbo Forsey's brother. He married Eleanor Lake (1880-1961) of Fortune

I would like to be able to drop in to-night and have tea, a regular feed on meat & potatoes.

I have an Xray of my ankle & I'll try and get it from the Doctor and send it to you a little later for a souvenir.

With best wishes for a happy Xmas.

I remain Your Son,
Curtis

---

and they were the parents of Eric, Margaret, Charles and Chesley. He was a founding partner, with his brother-in-law Charles Forward (see note 128), of Forward & Tibbo, which began business in 1908.

Bletchingley Castle Relief Hosp.
Bletchingley
Surrey
Nov 29/18

Dear Mother,

I wrote father a few days ago & yesterday I received his letter of Oct 30 in which he said he had not heard from me since I was wounded.

I really don't understand as as soon as I got in hosp. in France I wrote & upon arriving in England I wrote again so I suppose they must have been mislaid somewhere.

I guess by now you are enjoying Xmas. I was thinking last Xmas when I was in Scotland, if I would ever live to see next Xmas. Well after so many narrow escapes I have & I guess I'll hang on all right until then.

I am so glad to think that Sam will never have to come over & fight. Really I believe if he should ever come I'd go crazy. I can't bear to think of him being in the trenches, as I'd know he'd suffer awfully.

The "flu"[153] certainly seems to be all over the world doesn't it.

---

153. The Spanish influenza pandemic, the most destructive pandemic in recorded history, caused the deaths of somewhere between 50 and 100 million people during the years 1918 to 1920, compared with approximately 20 million deaths that occurred during the war. The pandemic did not start in Spain but acquired that descriptor because Spain observed neutrality during the war, and as a result there was much wider reporting of world news, since there was no wartime censorship on the Spanish press. The first known occurence of

People were dying in London wholesale, but I think they are getting it under control now. Father said Geo Dunford[154] was very low with it. Several patients died with it when I was in London Hosp.

You can see that I am still at Convalescent. I expect to go sometime next week.

Father said that Rheub Osmond was reported missing. Well as I said the piece of shell that wounded me killed him. I saw him fall and other boys in his section told me he was killed instantly. Now don't say that as if he is reported missing let it be so. But he is dead all right. Of course while he [is] reported missing his people get his money, while as soon as he is reported killed the money stops.

I don't know what happened to Lench, I'm sure. I haven't heard from him for a long time. I should feel awfully cut up if he should go west, but I suppose no more for one than another.

I wrote Sam & Christie yesterday. Tell Sam to hurry up & write me as I'm tired of writing him & getting no answer. With best wishes for a Merry Xmas & Happy New Year.

> I remain Your affect. Son
> Curtis

---

of the disease was at Fort Riley, Kansas, USA, March 11, 1918. It spread easily among the troops in Europe because of the frequent movement of large numbers of troops, their close living quarters, and their weakened immune systems caused by the stresses of battle, physical injuries and deficient diets.

154. George Forsey Samuel Dunford (1876–1960) survived his bout of the Spanish flu and lived to be 84. A native of Grand Bank, he married Emily Harris (1880–1948), a daugher of Mary Forsey and Samuel Harris (see note 83), and they were the parents of two children, Barbara and Chesley. Employed for many years with the Samuel Harris Export Company and its successor, Grand Bank Fisheries Limited, he served as directors of both companies. A member of Fidelity Masonic Lodge, his record of 13 terms as Worshipful Master has not been surpassed. He died on August 12, 1960.

KING GEORGE & QUEEN MARY'S CLUB
FOR THE OVERSEA FORCES[155]

                          Peel House
                          Regency Street
                          London. S.W.
                          Dec. 11/18

Dear Father,

I received mother's and Ches's letter yesterday and was indeed glad to hear from home once more.

I must now thank you for your kindness in sending me the six pounds I wired for. I assure you I appreciate it very much indeed.

The reason I wired for eight afterwards was that I thought

---

155. King George & Queen Mary's Club for the Oversea Forces was located at Peel House, 105 Regency Street in Westminster, London. It belonged to the Metropolitan Police whose Commissioner, Sir Edward Henry, made it available in 1915 as a recreation centre for non-commissioned officers (lance corporals, corporals and sergeants) from the various Empire forces. It provided single and dormitory sleeping accommodations for 400 men, who were able to avail of hot baths, a barbershop, large dining room, billiards room, writing room and library. Theatre tickets, excursions in and around London and the surrounding countryside and other activities were provided at no charge. Four small river craft, appropriately named *Maple Leaf*, *Terra Nova*, *Anzac* and *Springbok*, allowed for boating on the Thames. As the London *Times* for July 8, 1916, reported: "Peel House is, in its way an Imperial centre; for here, as experience shows, Canadian makes friends with Australian, and South African with Newfoundlander . . . drawing closer the bonds of union."

you had not received my first message, and when I saw you had a message paid for me to send why I cabled back for the eight pounds.

You can see I am now on leave for a few days. I expect to go back to Winchester on the 15th. Just too late to catch a draft of 300 going home. Well I'll get the next boat I suppose.

I hear they are sending another boat in January so I'll get that one. My wounds are quite healed up now and I have no difficulty whatever in walking.

Mother I'm afraid worried more than was necessary over me as I can just imagine how she took it while you were waiting for my letters to come.

She said that you had received them from hospital so of course you knew everything was OK.

Sam I suppose is still at Burin.

I shall be glad indeed to get out of this country. I don't think I could ever live here.

Jack Patten I think had to stay in France with his wound, as it wasn't much. I'm mighty glad I got to Blighty. If I didn't I suppose I would be on the German border now.

I will write again in a few days and I guess will be able to give you some idea when I shall be leaving for home.

I remain Your Affectionate Son,
Curtis

"H" Coy
Hazeley Down Camp
Winchester
Dec. 18 [1918]

Dear Mother,

I wrote father about 10 days ago, while I was in London. Since then I have received no word from home. The reason I didn't write before was that I waited for some mail. But I am writing tonight anyway as I suppose the mail has been mislaid.

I got back to camp Sunday Dec 15/ after a very nice time indeed in London.

I got back just too late to see Joe Harris[156] before he left for home. I would very much liked to have seen him but I suppose I'll get back myself by the next boat.

Although they say that they are going to keep all A^1 men until the last, and of course I'm A^1 so I may not get back as soon as I might expect.

However, I guess it will not be long now and as there is no more France for me I don't worry.

---

156. Private Josiah Harris (1899–1960), Newfoundland Regiment #2972, the son of Maria and George Harris of Grand Bank. The family also included sisters Mary, Emily, and Myrtle (1905–2003), who married John Francis, and brother Ira. He was one of several members of the Regiment who were taken prisoner of war at Monchy in mid-April 1917 and spent the following 17 months in a German prisoner of war camp. He returned to Grand Bank for a few years after the war, but later moved to Buffalo, New York, where he worked as a painting contractor. He married Grace Johnson of Eden, New York, and they were the parents of two sons, Joseph and Frank. He died at Buffalo, New York.

Sam I am glad kept out of it. I'm afraid he could never have stuck it.

Rog Lench I am glad got through it OK and Jack Patten I suppose is back with the boys as I heard he did not get to England. He certainly had a narrow escape.

How is all the family. Ches and Eleanor I suppose still go to school, and by the time you get this Xmas will be all over. I was thinking today how many Xmas's I have been from home & I counted six.

Just think I haven't been home for four this time.

Things seem to be very dead around here as most of the boys are gone home from the depot.

I am anxiously expecting Mrs. King's[157] parcel. I think I told you I heard from Mr. King while I was a convalescent. The parcel has not yet arrived. I hope it does not go astray.

I have received no parcel for a long time. Oh when I next get home and have a square meal of good clean and well cooked food I suppose I'll do as father says - make a glutton of myself.

But I'm afraid I won't have appetite enough as I eat hardly anything now. One slice of bread for tea and breakfast is plenty for me now.

It's surprising how little food one can thrive on.

Weather as usual here is wet & damp and I don't think it was ever any better.

I remain Your loving Son
Curtis

P. S. You may address my next letters as above.

---

157. The couple referred to here is probably Sarah Forsey King (1889-1975) and John King (1879-1954) of Fortune.

Dec. 27th 1918
Hazeley Down Camp, Winchester

Dear Mother,

I have received no letters from home since I came back from hospital. I really don't know why no mail has come for me. I am anxiously awaiting a letter.

Things are practically the same around here - very slow and not many of the boys here now as they are nearly all going home and are on leave. I expect to go home myself sometime in Jany, I guess about the last. We had a very poor Xmas indeed here. I never felt so miserable in all my life. It was absolutely a dead affair. Geo Wooden[158] & Billy Pennell are here with us. They were going to France but I think it is cancelled.

It's great to be back once more from France. You meet boys every day that you thought were killed. I met a chap yesterday. He was so surprised to see me. He said I thought you were dead. I heard you were killed last April. I feel sorry now that I got wounded

---

158. Private George Wooden (1897–1922), Newfoundland Regiment #5575, of Grand Bank. He was the son of Carrie and Thomas Wooden. He survived the war and returned to Grand Bank, but later moved to Lamaline where he died in 1922. Robert (1897–1918), George's brother, was a driver with the 6th Brigade of the Canadian Field Artillery. He was killed at Bramshott, England, on October 28, 1918, while driving a tank, and is buried at Bramshott (St. Mary) Churchyard. Their grandfather, Benjamin Wooden (or Benjamin de Wolfe, as he was also known), who came to Grand Bank from Nova Scotia some time around 1860, was reputed to be of Micmac descent.

as, if I walk any distance my leg gives out, but I suppose that will be all right in a few weeks.

Sometimes I feel I'd like to be on the Rhine yet with the boys & see what Germany looked like, but I suppose it is for the best as perhaps had I not got wounded when I did I could have gone west so I suppose it is all right as it turned out.

I hear Rog Lench is safe I hope he is any way. Sam I suppose is getting on well at Epworth.

I received Mrs. King's parcel yesterday. I was very glad indeed to get it. It was a nice parcel indeed.

You will have to excuse this writing as I can only get two sheets and there are no pens here & I only have a stump of a pencil.

I remain Your Affectionate Son,
Curtis

"H" Company
Hazeley Down Camp
Winchester
Jan 2/19

Dear Mother,

At last I received a letter from home. It was one of yours written Dec 12/ in which you said Ben's[159] body would be on the boat.

I didn't know he was dead until yesterday when Geo Wooden told me.

This is the first letter I received from home since I left hospital.

I was sorry to hear Ches was ill but I suppose he is well again by this time.

So Sam doesn't like his job Eh?

Well I suppose it is a bit slow for a young boy like him, but still he has got a good job there and ought to take advantage of it.

I suppose I shall go back to Waterbury again when I get home. I think I can get a job with the same people I was with before.

They say that there is a boat leaving sometime this month for Nfld. I hope they let me go on her. I am sick of this country.

---

159. Benjamin Lawrence Woundy (1895-1918), the son of Elizabeth Lawrence and James Woundy of Grand Bank, was a Cadet with the Royal Air Force (42nd Wing). Before enlisting he had been employed with the Bank of Nova Scotia at its branch in Havana, Cuba. He died at Quinte Hospital in Belleville, Ontario, on November 29, 1918, eighteen days after the end of the war, a victim of the Spanish 'flu' epidemic. His body was returned to Newfoundland and is buried in Grand Bank United Church Cemetery.

So Miss Shaw wrote you for my address did she.

I met her while I was in Waterbury and she has sent me three or four parcels since I went to France. I received one yesterday from her. She writes me quite often. I didn't know she knew your name. I never remember telling her but I suppose she must have known.

I also got Mrs. King's parcel as well so you see I was lucky New Year's. I haven't received one from home since I was in hospital but I suppose they must be where my letters are.

New Year's I may say was just as dull as Xmas. I never struck such a dump in my life – 4 miles from any town. Just imagine what you have to put up with when you are in the army.

The quicker I get out of the army the better so when I come home I want you to have a suit of civies all pressed up waiting for me, also a shirt & collar and tie. Don't forget.

> I remain Your loving Son,
> Curtis

"H" Coy
Royal Nfld Regt
Hazeley Down Camp
Winchester
8/1/19

Dear Mother,

I received a letter today written October 31. No doubt it has just about been all over Europe, however, it finally got here.

About three days ago I got four. They were written Nov 21 and Dec 6 and dates between.

You spoke on them about coming home, well I cannot say when I'm sure. I heard to-day a boat was sailing January 23/ w[h]ether I will go on that one or not I don't know. I'm really anxious to go home, but that winter trip across is not very comfortable especially on a troop ship. Any way, I hope I do. There are about 250 or 300 going so I think I might to stand a chance among so many. No doubt Joe Harris has safely arrived home before this. I think I heard they were home for Xmas.

Yes Lench is safe & sound so I heard & also Jack, he wasn't so lucky as I was. I am certainly proud of my scars, four of them.

I often wonder if I am still alive, sometimes I think about it and wonder how I ever escaped with my life. There has been times when I just sat in the trench and waited to die as there seemed no escape, but somehow I managed to escape.

Things are quite dull indeed around here. It is almost as bad as France. In fact, it is not so lively.

Geo Tibbo is around here yet. Just the same old George, cap on one side. Him & I often go out for a walk and talk over things. He laughs every time he speaks about his father getting converted.

I have not received Hettie's or Aunt Win's parcel. I think I told you I got Mrs. King's. I wrote her immediately after I received it. It was certainly very nice of her. I also received one from that Miss Shaw you spoke of the day before New Year's, so you see I wasn't so bad off after all. I would certainly like to get Aunt Min's as I know there is something good in it. Sam I suppose is the same old go. I think he must find it lonely. Anyway when I come home I will go down & see him for a few days.

I was sorry to hear Ches was sick by your letter but I suppose he is better now.

Poor Ben Woundy. I told Geo Tibbo he was dead & he said "Damn it he owes me $2."

Guess I [will] close for now with kind regards to everybody. Tell father to write once in awhile.

Your loving Son,
Curtis

Winchester
13/1/19

Dear Father

Have received no letter from home since writing last. No doubt this will be my last letter from here as I am leaving a week from to-day for home. Perhaps I shall be home anyway before this.

I think I wrote mother a few days ago. I haven't heard from you for a long long time. I suppose though you have been busy.

Great to hear on the last letter that the family was all well.

I don't know what they will do with us when we get home. I don't think we will be discharged until peace is signed so I shall have a little soldiering in Nfld. It's better than France anyway.

Ben Lee I think is coming with us. He is the one Gr Banker besides me that is coming. I dread the passage across but I'm going home again & it won't matter much.

I won't bore you with a long letter this time as perhaps I shall be home before this arrives.

I remain Your Son
Curtis

NEWFOUNDLAND POSTAL TELEGRAPHS

St. John's   8 F[ebruary] '19

To   Mr. William Forsey
                G Bank

Arrived today coming on Glencoe.[160]

                Curtis

---

160. One of the original vessels known as the Alphabet Fleet that were used to supplement the Newfoundland rail system. The SS *Glencoe* was the chief coastal boat used for the Placentia and Fortune Bay runs.

APPENDIX

GRAND BANKERS WHO SERVED IN WORLD WAR I

The men listed below served in World War I. Most of them were born in Grand Bank. Those who were not either spent most of life before the war living there or had some other connection to the town. The list for the Royal Newfoundland Regiment is thought to be complete. The others may not be and there is no list for the Royal Naval Reserve or for British regiments in which Grand Bankers may have served. Any additional information about any of these men will be greatly appreciated and can be forwarded to Bert Riggs, PO Box 2027, St. John's, NL A1C 5R6 (email: briggs@mun.ca; telephone 709-737-6169).

ROYAL NEWFOUNDLAND REGIMENT

	Name		Regimental Number	Rank	Birth and death dates
1.	Barnes	George	(4636)	Pte	(October 2, 1895–April 13, 1982)
2.	Bennett[1]	George Graham	(2888)	Pte	(May 19, 1897–July 31, 1964)
3.	Bennett	Thomas	(4084)	Pte	(February 25, 1899–19??)
4.	Clarke[2]	George Max	(2973)	Cpl	(May 19, 1897–April 18, 1918)
5.	Coxworthy[3]	Charles Frederick Pierre	(1304)	Pte	(October 25, 1895–January 15, 1983)
6.	Coxworthy[4]	Frank	(1820)	Pte	(July 28, 1898–August 10, 1979)
7.	Douglas[5]	Aaron Keeping	(2904)	Pte	(18??–September 29, 1918)
8.	Evans	Joseph	(2793)	Pte	(September 20, 1897–June 1975)
9.	Follett[6]	Albert	(2920)	Pte	(1896–April 14, 1917)
10.	Forsey	Claude	(2971)	Pte	(November 3, 1895–October 20, 1993)
11.	Forsey	Curtis	(3828)	L/C	(June 28, 1900–1948)
12.	Fox	William T.	(5797)	Pte	(December 24, 1898–January 27, 1960)
13.	Harris[7]	Josiah	(2972)	Pte	(April 19, 1896–May 1, 1982)
14.	Hause	John O.	(4324)	Pte	(March 6, 1895–September 21, 1964)
15.	Hollett	Samuel	(3877)	Pte	(March 30, 1900–19??)
16.	Lee	Benjamin John	(4082)	Pte	

152

17.	Lee	Ernest	(4171)	Pte	(September 13, 1900–19??)
18.	Lee	George James	(5875)	Pte	(1894–September 17, 1968)
19.	Lench[8]	James Rogerson	(3862)	Pte	(November 08, 1896–July 12, 1954)
20.	Lench[9]	William Herbert	(1122)	Sgt	(November 28, 1894–February 22, 1938)
21.	Nicholle	Edward Henry	(664)	CQMS	(September 17, 1892–October 10, 1917)
22.	Osborne	Reuben	(3421)	Pte	(March 13, 1898–September 29, 1918)
23.	Patten	John Benjamin	(3831)	L/C	(March 4, 1896–June 23, 1980)
24.	Penwell	William John	(4583)	Pte	(July 12, 1886–April 4, 1988)
25.	Purchase	Abia Arthur	(2995)	Pte	(July 23, 1876–August 31, 1961)
26.	Riggs	George	(4085)	Pte	(November 4, 1895–August 8, 1959)
27.	Riggs	Leslie Rose	(1106)	Sgt	(August 19, 1891–June 9, 1937)
28.	Riggs	Morgan	(5598)	Pte	(December 2, 1893–December 1, 1962)
29.	Riggs	Rennie	(3721)	Sgt	(December 12, 1895–May 11, 1930)
30.	Snook	Thomas	(6042)	Pte	(January 11, 1898–June 10, 1987)
31.	Stoodley	Lyman	(2160)	Pte	(1897–August 18, 1917)
32.	Thorne	Joseph	(3149)	Pte	(May 14, 1897–December 17, 1917)
33.	Tibbo	George Philip	(634)	Cpl	(September 05, 1886–1961)
34.	Weymouth	Berkley	(4081)	Pte	(August 15, 1890–1938)
35.	Wooden	George	(5575)	Pte	(December 3, 1895–September 15, 1922)

1. Born in St. John's; lived in Grand Bank from age 5.
2. Born in Bonavista but lived in Grand Bank from age 1.
3. Born in St. Pierre; lived in Grand Bank from age 5 to 16.
4. Born in St. Pierre; lived in Grand Bank from age 2 to 8.
5. Born Brunette Island; name appears on Grand Bank War Memorial.
6. Born Grand Beach; name appears on Grand Bank War Memorial.
7. Prisoner of War from April 14, 1917 to November 29, 1918.
8. Born Bay Roberts; lived in Grand Bank during part of his father's term as Methodist minister (1912–1916).
9. Born in Greenspond; lived in Grand Bank during part of his father's term as Methodist minister (1912–1916); lists Grand Bank as his place of residence on his enlistment form.

Canadian Expeditionary Force

#	Surname	Given names	Service #	Dates
1.	Courtney	Henry James	(1258180)	(December 7, 1898–19??)
2.	Evans	Isaac	(472513)	(September 20, 1893–19??)
3.	Forsey	George Aaron	(113227)	(September 30, 1892–19??)
4.	Forsey	George Edward	(113222)	((September 30, 1983–June 2, 1916)
5.	Hickman	Charles Forsey	(871526)	(October 9, 1893–April 12, 1917)
6.	Hickman	Chesley Lloyd	(409533)	(June 13, 1896–19??)
7.	Hickman	Harold	(3040975)	(September 8, 1889–19??)
8.	Hickman	Percival	(2115242)	(October 15, 1886–March 25, 1966)
9.	Hickman	Wilson Jonathan	(902211)	(August 14, 1884–February 15, 1917)
10.	Janes	Robert Bond	(3182676)	(March 4, 1894–19??)
11.	MacDonald	Norman Stanley	(248489)	(October 10, 1894–November 24, 1962)
12.	Millington	Samuel	(68408)	(April 18, 1893–19??)
13.	Pardy	William	(769718)	(October 6, 1896–19??)
14.	Patten	Edward	(514053)	(October 13, 1887–19??)
15.	Patten	Eli Harris	(540027)	(December 13, 1893–September 1, 1916)
16.	Patten	James	(669865)	(September 1891–19??)
17.	Patten	John Forsey	(669802)	(November 22, 1889–19??)
18.	Patten	Lewis Edwin	(33993)	(October 3, 1890–19??)
19.	Patten	Robert Forsey	(3033952)	(December 22, 1889–19??)
20.	Pugh	Evan William	(655609)	(June 28, 1894–August 22, 1918)
21.	Riggs	Samuel	(2125044)	(June 12, 1892–November 9, 1971)
22.	Rose	James Charles	(9953)	(November 15, 1883–19??)
23.	Rose	James Robert	(469143)	(June 6, 1894–1966)
24.	Rose	John Hickman	(503999)	(April 4, 1871–19??)
25.	Tibbo	Aaron Grandy	(469152)	(September 3, 1892–April 30, 1948)
26.	Tibbo	George William	(3190730)	(May 22, 1891–19??)

Royal Air Force

1. Woundy Benjamin (171339) (November 10, 1895–November 29, 1918)

Royal Medical Corps

1. Harris Chester (July 10, 1887–August 19 1971)

Newfoundland Forestry Corps

1. Dodman Leslie (8146) Pte (October ??, 1898–September 3, 1937)

Borders Regiment (British)

1. Curtis Pierson Vivian (April 25, 1893–January 1, 1961)

BIBLIOGRAPHY

Atlantic Guardian, Vol. VI (1), January 1949, pp. 41-51.

Commonwealth War Graves Commission [website: http://www.cwgc.org].

Cramm, Richard. *The First Five Hundred*. Albany, NY: C. F. Williams & Son, Inc., [1921].

Fidelity Lodge: The Centenary of Fidelity Lodge No. 1659 A.F. & A.M. Grand Bank Newfoundland 1876-1976. [Grand Bank: Fidelity Lodge, 1976].

Fizzard, Garfield. *Unto the Sea*. Grand Bank: Grand Bank Heritage Society, 1987.

Hibbs, Richard. *Who's Who In and From Newfoundland 1927*. St. John's, R. Hibbs, 1927.

Library and Archives of Canada. "Soldiers of the First World War" [website: http://www.collectionscanada.ca/archivianet/cef/001042-100.01-e.html].

Milley, Hazel. "The Forseys of Grand Bank, Newfoundland: A Scrapbook." [unpublished].

Nicholson, G. W. L. *The Fighting Newfoundlander*. St. John's: Government of Newfoundland, [1964].

Parsons, Robert C. *Vignettes of a Small Town*. St. John's: Creative Publishers, 1997.

Parsons, W. David. *The Pilgrimage: A Guide to the Royal Newfoundland Regiment in World War One*. St. John's: Creative, 1994.

ScotiaBank Group Archives.

The Veteran, Vol. 4 (1), April 1924, p. 50.

Yearbook and Almanac of Newfoundland. St. John's: King's Printer, 1902–1920.

ACKNOWLEDGEMENTS

Many people have contributed to the making of this book. Mary Philpott, the fount of all knowledge on Newfoundland VADs and nurses in World War I, was always willing to assist in my research efforts, for which I am incredibly grateful. The Hon. T. Alex Hickman generously agreed to write the foreword and shared his memories of growing up in Grand Bank with me on many occasions. Anne Patten Oliver, whose vast database of Grand Bank genealogies, especially Pattens and Forseys, is second to none, responded to my plaintive e-mails promptly and cheerfully, providing vital information.

At Memorial University, Heather Wareham of the Maritime History Archive went the extra nautical mile to solve the mystery of the *Tuscania*. Shannon Gordon of the Queen Elizabeth II Library's Information Services division discovered a very pertinent piece of information while Joan Ritcey of the Centre for Newfoundland Studies not only contributed her expertise as a reference librarian but was also a constant source of encouragement. To all my colleagues at the Queen Elizabeth II Library and especially to Gail Weir and Linda White, with whom I work on a daily basis, thank you for putting up with me and helping to make my job such a delight.

I owe an immense debt of gratitude to Christina Trastelis of the ScotiaBank Group Archives, 44 King Street West, Toronto, Ontario. She arranged for the reproductions of the photographs of Graham Bennett, Max Clarke and Benjamin Woundy that appear in this volume to be copied and supplied to me. She also provided me with information about each of these men from the ScotiaBank Group Archives files, which has been integrated into the brief biographical sketches that appear as notes 42, 55, and 159 in the text. I very much appreciate the willingness of ScotiaBank Group Archives to provide me with access to and permission to use this material.

On the picture front, in Grand Bank, my sister, Margaret Prior acted as intermediary with Rosalind Robere to locate the image of Reuben Osborne, and with Margaret Follett for a picture of her father, George Riggs, while Ethel Brown searched through family photos for the appropriate picture of her uncle, William J. Penwell; General John L. Patten of Middletown, Pennsylvania, sent the picture of his father, John B. Patten; Edward Coxworthy of Bell Island and Fred Coxworthy of St. John's both supplied copies of the picture of their father Pierre, with Fred also providing several missing pieces of the puzzle regarding the Coxworthy family and Grand Bank.

Robert and Sadie Parsons of Grand Bank were very supportive: Robert was always ready to answer any question I might have and Sadie made arrangements for a launch of the book as part of the Grand Bank Come Home Year 2007 festivities. Randy Dawe of Randy Dawe Photography and Framing, St. John's, copied and enhanced many of the images used here and his wife and business partner, Victoria Dawe, was an enthusiastic booster of the project from day one.

The wonderful people at Flanker Press treated this project with their usual high degree of professionalism. To publisher Garry Cranford, marketing dynamo Margo Cranford and copy editor Jerry Cranford, I express my sincere appreciation for their confidence in me and their commitment to publishing in this province. To my production editor, Dwayne LaFitte, I can honestly say what a great pleasure it is to work with you; and to graphic designer Adam Freake, thank you for another marvellous cover.

Members of Curt and Hazel Forsey's family have been my keenest and staunchest supporters for this book. Their grandson, Dr. Robert Forsey, of Happy Valley—Goose Bay, provided me with both the actual letters and typed transcriptions to work from and a copy of a Forsey family scrapbook compiled by his cousin Hazel Milley. From her home base in Montreal, Hazel was never more than an e-mail or telephone call away. She cheerfully accepted my research enquiries and came back with the answers in jig time and sent copies of many of the Forsey family photographs found in the book. Helen Forsey Milley, Curt and Hazel's oldest child, was one of the first people to whom I broached the idea of a book of her father's letters: as soon as she recovered from the surprise, she became my Muse and my Mentor. To her I owe my sincerest thanks for her trust in me and her unqualified encouragement and support.

>
> Bert Riggs
> St. John's
> May 25, 2007

ABOUT THE EDITOR

Bert Riggs, who was born in Grand Bank, Newfoundland, in 1954, holds a B.A. and a B.Ed. from Memorial University and a masters degree in information studies from the University of Toronto. He has been an archivist at Memorial University since 1989 and currently is head of the Archives and Manuscripts Division of the university's Queen Elizabeth II Library. From 1997 to 2006, he wrote a weekly column for the St. John's *Telegram*. He is a bencher with the Law Society of Newfoundland and Labrador and is chair of the board of the Resource Centre for the Arts, owners and operators of the LSPU Hall. In 2006, he collaborated with Senator William Rompkey to produce *Your Daughter Fanny: The War Letters of Frances Cluett, VAD*, also published by Flanker Press.

RELATED INTEREST

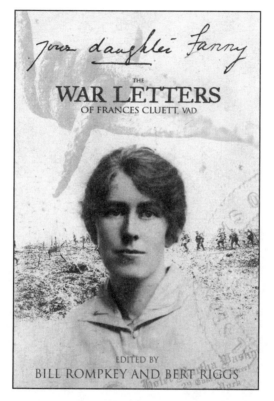

EDITED BY BILL ROMPKEY AND BERT RIGGS

Frances Cluett was born in Belleoram, Newfoundland, in 1883. At the age of thirty-three, she left her Fortune Bay home to join the Voluntary Aid Detachment (VAD), an organization committed to assisting military personnel during World War I. She trained in London, England, for work in a military hospital and in 1917 was stationed at the 10th General Hospital in Rouen, France.

During her four years of service overseas, Nurse Cluett wrote many letters to home. Contained here are the war letters she sent to her mother in Newfoundland, telegrams describing the atrocities of war, the valiant deeds of comrades in arms, and the despair of young men dying on foreign shores.

ISBN 13: 978-1-894463-92-8 $14.95   172 pages